Better Homes and Gardens

ENCYCLOPEDIA
of
COOKING

Volume 3

Prepare chopped broccoli in a puffy mixture. The creamy Mushroom Sauce, spooned over individual servings, completes this main dish Broccoli Soufflé—perfect for a luncheon.

On the cover: When holiday baking plans include a fruitcake, try one with a different twist. Dublin Fruitcake sports a double topping—first a layer of almond paste, then Royal Icing.

BETTER HOMES AND GARDENS BOOKS
NEW YORK • DES MOINES

BROCCOLI—A vegetable of the cauliflower family, related to the cabbage, falling into two basic categories: (1) Italian or sprouting; and (2) heading or cauliflower. The broccoli stems, buds, and a few of the leaves are the edible parts.

Although the history of sprouting broccoli pre-dates Christianity, the use of broccoli as a vegetable in the United States is recent. For more than 200 years its use on the American continent was largely confined to the Italian-born populations of the New York and Boston areas where broccoli was grown in home vegetable gardens for consumption at the family table.

The introduction of the delicate autumn and spring vegetable to hotels and restaurants in the early 1920s coincided with a trial planting in the Santa Clara Valley of California. From these two occurrences broccoli emerged as a major vegetable on the American market. Now the vegetable is grown in areas across the United States —California, Arizona, New Jersey, New York, Oregon, Pennsylvania, South Carolina, Texas, and Virginia.

Sprouting broccoli is the beautiful deep green vegetable that is most familiar in American markets, and tastes more like cabbage. It has branching clusters of buds on a thick stalk growing 2 to 2½ feet tall.

The less familiar type, heading broccoli, differs from sprouting in that while it doesn't taste exactly like cauliflower it has a similar appearance, with a large, white compact curd. This type of broccoli takes longer to reach maturity.

Nutritional value: Broccoli not only adds color to the menu but contains valuable nutrients. Two-thirds cup of cooked broccoli, including stalks and tops, has only 26 calories, but contributes half of the recommended daily allowance of vitamin A for adults, and about 1½ times the recommended adult daily allowance of vitamin C. It also contains some iron, some of the B vitamins, calcium, and potassium, and is a vegetable relatively low in sodium.

How to select: Fresh broccoli is available almost the entire year, except during the hot summer months. The main harvest is between October and March.

Choose broccoli that has firm, tender stalks that are fresh and clean and bear small, crisp leaves. The buds should be in compact clusters, tightly closed, showing no signs of flowering. The sizes of the heads vary, but this does not affect the eating quality. Depending on the variety, the vegetable should be from dark green to a purplish green. Yellow in the buds or woody stalks is a sign of poor quality, over maturity, and toughness.

Broccoli is also available year around in frozen forms—spears, cuts, and chopped, and also frozen with sauces.

How to store: Fresh broccoli should be loosely covered with foil or clear plastic wrap, or put into a plastic bag, then stored in crisper of the refrigerator. If uncooked, broccoli will keep one to two days in refrigerator; cooked broccoli stored tightly covered will keep one to four days.

To freeze broccoli, wash, peel stalks, and trim. Cut into medium pieces 5 to 6 inches long, no thicker than 1½ inches. Blanch in boiling water 3 minutes, or steam on rack over boiling water 5 minutes. Package in moisture-vaporproof containers. Seal, label, and freeze.

How to prepare: Trim off a piece from the base of the broccoli stalk, then rinse thoroughly under cold water. Place in about 1 inch of boiling, salted water, cover, and cook 10 to 15 minutes, till tender. When stalks are thicker than 1 inch in diameter, make 4 or 5 lengthwise gashes almost to buds (flowerets) before cooking. This allows the stalks of the broccoli to cook as quickly as the flowerets.

To steam whole spears: split stalk almost to flowerets and tie stalks in bundle using a folded strip of foil. Then stand the bundle in 1 inch boiling, salted water in a saucepan. Cover and cook 15 to 20 minutes, till stalks are tender.

An alternate and faster method is to cut stalks in 1-inch pieces and cook, covered, in boiling, salted water 5 to 8 minutes. Add flowerets and cook 5 to 7 additional minutes. Then drain the cooked broccoli.

Avoid overcooking broccoli. Excess cooking results in an unattractive color change from green to olive green by breaking down the chlorophyll pigment when it merges with the volatile acids. When an acid food, such as vinegar or lemon juice, is added for flavor, it is best to add it to the broccoli just before serving.

How to use: Use broccoli in main dish casseroles. Combine it with bacon, poultry, ham, and seafood. You can also use it in soufflés, or with butter as a vegetable.

Broccoli Soufflé

An elegant main dish—

> 1 10-ounce package frozen
>   chopped broccoli
> 2 tablespoons butter or margarine
> 2 tablespoons all-purpose flour
> ½ teaspoon salt
> ½ cup milk
> ¼ cup grated Parmesan cheese
> 4 egg yolks
> 4 stiffly beaten egg whites
>   • • •
>   **Mushroom Sauce**

Cook broccoli following package directions. Drain *very thoroughly*. (Chop large pieces.) Add butter to broccoli; cook and stir over high heat till butter is melted and moisture is evaporated. Reserve 2 tablespoons broccoli for top; set aside. Blend in flour and salt; add milk all at once. Cook and stir over medium heat till mixture thickens and bubbles. Remove from heat; stir in Parmesan cheese.

Beat egg yolks till thick and lemon colored. Add broccoli mixture to egg yolks, stirring constantly. Pour over egg whites; fold together thoroughly. Pour into *ungreased* 1-quart soufflé dish. Bake at 350° for 20 minutes. Ring soufflé top with reserved 2 tablespoons broccoli. Bake 15 minutes longer or till knife inserted comes out clean. Serve with hot Mushroom Sauce. Makes 4 to 6 servings.

Mushroom Sauce: Lightly brown 1 pint fresh mushrooms *or* one 6-ounce can sliced mushrooms, drained, in ¼ cup melted butter. Blend in 2 tablespoons all-purpose flour and dash *each* salt and pepper. Add 1 cup water and 1 chicken bouillon cube; cook and stir till sauce thickens and bubbles. Stir in 1 tablespoon chopped canned pimiento. Cook 1 to 2 minutes longer.

Turkey Parisian

> 2 tablespoons chopped green pepper
> ¼ cup butter or margarine
> ¼ cup all-purpose flour
> ¾ teaspoon salt
> 1½ cups milk
> 1 cup light cream
> 2 cups cubed cooked turkey
> 1 3-ounce can sliced mushrooms,
>   drained (½ cup)
> 1 5-ounce can lobster, broken into
>   bite-size pieces
> ¼ cup grated Parmesan cheese
> 2 tablespoons chopped canned
>   pimiento
> 2 tablespoons dry white wine
> 2 10-ounce packages frozen chopped
>   broccoli, cooked and drained

Cook green pepper in butter till tender. Blend in flour, salt, and dash pepper. Add milk and cream; cook, stirring constantly, till mixture thickens and bubbles. Stir in turkey, mushrooms, lobster, cheese, pimiento, and wine.

Place cooked broccoli in a 12x7½x2-inch baking dish. Top with turkey mixture. Sprinkle additional cheese atop, if desired. Bake at 350° for 30 to 35 minutes. Makes 8 servings.

Casserole À La King

> 1 10½-ounce can chicken à la king
> 1 10½-ounce can condensed cream
>   of celery soup
> 3 ounces sharp process American
>   cheese, shredded (¾ cup)
> 1 teaspoon prepared mustard
> ½ teaspoon curry powder
> ½ teaspoon Worcestershire sauce
> 2 cups uncooked fine noodles
> 1 10-ounce package frozen
>   broccoli spears

Heat first 6 ingredients till cheese is melted, stirring often. Cook noodles in boiling *unsalted* water till tender. Cook broccoli in boiling salted water till just tender.

Drain noodles and broccoli. Place noodles in greased 10x6x1½-inch baking dish. Arrange broccoli spears atop the noodles; pour chicken mixture over all. Bake at 375° for 10 to 15 minutes or till hot. Makes 4 servings.

For a change, try broccoli as a relish or salad. Use the raw flowerets with or without a zesty dip as a relish. (Reserve the stems to use in a creamy broccoli soup.) Or, cooked broccoli marinated in salad dressing makes a tasty salad as do raw flowerets added to a tossed green salad or in combination with tomato. Cooked broccoli is also delicious in a molded salad.

Creamy Broccoli Mold

      1 envelope (1 tablespoon) unflavored
        gelatin
    ¾ cup cold water
      1 10-ounce package frozen chopped
        broccoli
      2 chicken bouillon cubes
      1 tablespoon instant minced onion
              • • •
    ½ cup dairy sour cream
    ½ cup chopped celery
    ¼ cup chopped canned pimiento
      2 tablespoons snipped parsley
      2 tablespoons lemon juice

Soften gelatin in cold water. Cook broccoli according to package directions, adding bouillon cubes and onion. *Do not add salt. Do not drain.*

Add softened gelatin; stir to dissolve. Combine broccoli mixture with sour cream, celery, pimiento, parsley, and lemon juice. Chill till partially set. Pour into 5½-cup ring mold; chill till firm. Unmold onto a lettuce-lined plate. Makes 6 to 8 servings.

Probably the most popular way to serve broccoli is as a vegetable. A variety of sauces can complement the appealing flavor of broccoli. Good flavor accents include curry-seasoned butter or almond butter. (See also *Vegetable*.)

Broccoli Specials

• Dot cooked fresh or frozen broccoli with butter, then drizzle with lemon juice.
• Try Hollandaise, cheese, or mustard sauce spooned over cooked broccoli.
• Top cooked broccoli spears with canned pimiento strips and shredded Swiss cheese.

Broccoli Puff

A light, fluffy cheese topper over broccoli—

      1 10-ounce package frozen cut
        broccoli
      1 10½-ounce can condensed cream
        of mushroom soup
      2 ounces sharp process American
        cheese, shredded (½ cup)
              • • •
    ¼ cup milk
    ¼ cup mayonnaise or salad
        dressing
      1 beaten egg
              • • •
    ¼ cup fine dry bread crumbs
      1 tablespoon butter or margarine,
        melted

Cook broccoli according to package directions, omitting salt in cooking water; drain thoroughly. Place broccoli cuts in 10x6x1½-inch baking dish. Stir together condensed soup and cheese. Gradually add milk, mayonnaise, and beaten egg to soup mixture, stirring till well blended. Pour over broccoli in baking dish.

Combine bread crumbs and melted butter; sprinkle evenly over soup in baking dish. Bake at 350° for 45 minutes or till crumbs are lightly browned. Makes 6 servings.

Broccoli Italienne

The sauce complements the flavor of broccoli—

      2 10-ounce packages frozen
        broccoli spears *or* 2 pounds
        fresh broccoli
    ½ teaspoon dried oregano leaves,
        crushed
    ½ cup mayonnaise or salad
        dressing
    ¼ cup shredded sharp process
        American cheese
      1 tablespoon milk

Cook broccoli till tender in boiling salted water to which oregano has been added. Drain thoroughly. In small heavy saucepan mix mayonnaise, cheese, and milk; stir over *low* heat till cheese melts and mixture is hot. Spoon over hot cooked broccoli. Makes 6 servings.

Broccoli Casserole

> 2 tablespoons butter or margarine, melted
> 2 tablespoons all-purpose flour
> 1 3-ounce package cream cheese, softened
> 1 ounce blue cheese, crumbled (¼ cup)
> 1 cup milk
> 2 10-ounce packages frozen chopped broccoli, cooked and drained
> ⅓ cup rich round crackers, crushed (about 10 crackers)

In large saucepan blend butter, flour, cream cheese, and blue cheese. Add milk. Cook and stir till mixture bubbles.

Stir in cooked broccoli. Turn into a 1-quart casserole. Top with cracker crumbs. Bake at 350° for 30 minutes. Makes 8 to 10 servings.

Broccoli-Corn Bake

> 1 10-ounce package frozen chopped broccoli, thawed
> 1 17-ounce can cream-style corn
> ¼ cup saltine cracker crumbs
> 1 beaten egg
> 2 tablespoons butter or margarine, melted
> 1 tablespoon instant minced onion
> ½ teaspoon salt
> Dash pepper
> ¼ cup saltine cracker crumbs
> 2 tablespoons butter or margarine, melted

In a 1½-quart casserole combine thawed broccoli, corn, ¼ cup cracker crumbs, egg, 2 tablespoons melted butter or margarine, instant minced onion, salt, and pepper. Blend remaining ¼ cup cracker crumbs and 2 tablespoons melted butter. Sprinkle over top. Bake at 350° for 45 minutes. Makes 6 servings.

Broccoli adds color to the meal

←Italian or sprouting broccoli is the most familiar type seen in today's markets. The stems, buds, and some leaves are edible.

Broccoli with Shrimp

> 1 4-ounce container whipped cream cheese with chives
> ¼ cup milk
> 1 10-ounce can frozen condensed cream of shrimp soup
> 2 teaspoons lemon juice
>   •   •   •
> 2 10-ounce packages frozen broccoli spears, cooked and drained
> Toasted slivered almonds

In saucepan blend cream cheese and milk. Add shrimp soup; heat and stir until soup is thawed and mixture is smooth. Heat through; add lemon juice. Pour over broccoli and sprinkle with almonds. Makes 6 servings.

Broccoli in Foil

Place two 10-ounce packages frozen broccoli spears on large square of double-thickness of heavy foil. Season with salt and pepper. Tuck in thin slices of lemon or sprinkle with 1 tablespoon lemon juice. Top with 2 or 3 generous pats of butter or margarine.

Bring edges of foil up and seal tightly with double fold, leaving a little space for expansion of steam. Heat over *hot* coals about 40 minutes, turning frequently. Serves 6 to 8.

Broccoli Parmesan

> 2 10-ounce packages frozen broccoli spears *or* 2 pounds fresh broccoli
> 2 tablespoons butter or margarine
> ¼ cup chopped onion
> 1 10½-ounce can condensed cream of chicken soup
> ⅔ cup milk
> ⅓ cup grated Parmesan cheese

Cook broccoli till tender in boiling *unsalted* water; drain thoroughly.

Meanwhile, melt butter or margarine in a saucepan. Add onion and cook till onion is tender but not brown. Blend in condensed cream of chicken soup, milk, and grated Parmesan cheese. Heat thoroughly. Serve sauce over hot cooked broccoli. Makes 6 to 8 servings.

Prepare steaks or chops for broiling by slitting the fat and membrane at one-inch intervals. This prevents curling edges.

Brush melted butter or an herb-oil mixture on lean cuts of meat for broiling. This keeps meat surface moist and adds flavor.

BROCHETTE *(brō shet')*—French name for a small skewer cut from wood, metal, or bamboo on which foods are strung for broiling. Foods cooked in this manner are termed "en brochette." (See also *Kabob*.)

BROIL—To cook foods by direct heat in a broiler oven, portable broiler, or over charcoal. Broiling is also referred to as grilling, particularly in connection with outdoor cookery. Pan broil designates foods cooked in a skillet or on a griddle lightly rubbed with fat to prevent sticking. No cover is used. Because of the very small amount of fat used, pan broiling differs in this way from conventional frying.

Broiling is a flavorful and nutritious method for cooking meat, fish, and poultry. Steaks and chops brown in their own juices. Additional fat often is not necessary although barbecue sauces or well-seasoned marinades are popular for the flavor they add. During broiling, the natural fat within the meat renders out and drips into the broiler pan. Generally, these drippings are not served. Since fish and poultry are relatively low in fat, melted butter or a special basting sauce is brushed over the surface of these foods not only for flavor but also to keep them moist while cooking and to promote even browning.

As could be expected, broiling is highly recommended as a cookery method when counting calories. Much of the meat fat drips away during cooking and the remainder can be trimmed before serving. Also, low calorie salad dressings can easily be used as basting sauces.

Foods to broil: Meats, fish, and poultry are the basic foods for the broiler. Tenderness is the key to selecting foods, especially meats. Tender cuts are essential because in broiling food cooks without a cover and the meat does not benefit from the tenderizing action of the steam that is present in a covered pan.

Meats are the most-frequently broiled foods. Fresh beef and lamb are chosen because tender steaks, chops, and ground meat patties can be cooked rare, medium, or well done. You can use packaged meat tenderizers and packaged or homemade marinades successfully on meats to increase the variety of cuts, particularly beef, that are tender enough for broiling.

Other meats rating high for broilability include tender, fresh pork chops, hamburgers, frankfurters, ham slices, and smoked sausages. However, veal is seldom broiled because it's so lean. Braising veal is more satisfactory than broiling.

Following close to meat in popularity are chicken halves, quarters, or pieces. In fact, the word broiler is built into the name of tender, young birds to indicate a prized cooking method for them.

Enjoying broiled fish steaks or fillets need not be limited to a camping trip or outdoor grill. An electric broiler or the broiler in your kitchen range cooks these beauties quickly since there's no need to turn the pieces. Broiled shrimp or lobster make elegant eating too.

Some foods such as cake toppings or buttered crumbs on casseroles are broiled only till browned and bubbly. Likewise, pineapple rings and canned peach halves are delicious browned in the broiler.

How to broil: First check the broiler instruction booklet so directions for specific equipment can be followed. In general, preheat the broiler, but remove the broiler pan so that the food is placed on a cold rack. Oil the rack when doing fish, applying only where the fish will touch the rack. Special techniques for meat include slitting the fat and membrane of a steak or chop at one-inch intervals to prevent the edges from curling. If the meat is particularly lean, a basting sauce is needed to keep the surface of the food from drying out. Salt or seasonings are sprinkled on just before the food is turned or when it is brought to the table.

Thickness of the food and the desired degree of doneness influences placement in the broiler. Foods should be placed far

Brown meat cubes or a pot roast slowly on all sides in two tablespoons melted fat. Dust meat with seasoned flour, if desired.

enough from the source of heat to allow for a rich, even browning of the surface while reaching the desired doneness in the center. Thick steaks or patties you want to serve well done should be placed lower in the broiler oven than their thinner, rarer counterparts. Actually, foods less than one inch thick, because they cook so quickly, are usually more juicy when panbroiled than when broiled. (See *Fish, Meat, Poultry* for additional information.)

BROILER-FRYER CHICKEN—A young, tender chicken weighing one and one-half to three and one-half pounds which is marketed when nine weeks old. It has little fat and a high proportion of flesh to bone, and is grown for high eating quality. A broiler-fryer chicken is marketed whole, split, quartered, or cut into smaller pieces. It is suitable for cooking by broiling, panfrying, roasting, barbecuing, and baking. (See also *Chicken.*)

BROOK TROUT—A freshwater fish of the salmon family, also known as a mountain trout or as a speckled trout because of the colorful specks on its sides. The overall color varies from a dark brown to a flashy silver depending upon the streams in which the fish lives. This favorite game fish thrives in cold, rapid streams and deep cold lakes. (See also *Trout.*)

BROTH—The liquid in which meat, poultry, vegetables, or any combination of these has been cooked. It is a thin, clear soup not to be confused with stock which is richer and more concentrated. Broth is used as a liquid ingredient in making sauces and gravies. A variety of canned broths is available in the market and an "instant" broth can also be prepared using bouillon cubes or meat extract concentrates.

BROWN—To cook food in a skillet, broiler, or oven so that the desired rich color on the outside develops. Browning contributes both aroma and flavor to the food. The crusty surface and moist interior are pleasing contrasts in color and texture. Before braising meat, it is coated with a seasoned flour mixture to intensify the brown color of the cooked meat.

BROWN AND SERVE—A convenience food which is partially baked by the manufacturer. The homemaker briefly rebakes and browns the food prior to serving it. Brown and serve products include French rolls, butterflake rolls, croissants, French bread, dinner rolls, and meats, such as sausage. Many of these foods are stored without refrigeration, however package directions should be noted for specific storage instructions. (See also *Quick Cookery*.)

BROWN BETTY—A delicious dessert of brown sugar, bread crumbs, and fruit, usually sliced or chopped apples. (See *Betty, Dessert* for additional information.)

BROWN BREAD—Any leavened bread made with a dark flour, such as whole wheat or rye, rather than the usual wheat flour. When also made with cornmeal and steamed, the bread is called Boston brown bread. Brown bread is sold in paper packages and in cans. (See also *Bread*.)

BROWN GRAVY—Any gravy made from the pan juices produced during the cooking of meat. Flour is used for thickening and water, milk, broth, or wine for the liquid.

Serve brown gravy over the meat and vegetables, or save it for use as an ingredient in casseroles and stews. When pan juices are not available, brown gravy mix or canned gravy can be used very successfully. (See also *Gravy*.)

Pan Gravy

Remove meat to hot platter and keep warm. Leaving crusty bits in roasting pan, pour meat juices and fat into large measuring cup. Skim off fat reserving 3 to 4 tablespoons. For 2 cups gravy, return reserved fat to pan. Stir in ¼ cup all-purpose flour. Blend together fat and flour. Cook and stir over low heat till mixture is thickened and bubbly.

Remove pan from the heat. Add 2 cups liquid (meat juices plus water, milk, or broth) all at once; stir to blend. Season with salt and pepper. If desired, add a dash of dried thyme, crushed, and a few drops kitchen bouquet. Simmer, stirring constantly, for 2 to 3 minutes. Serve with meat. Makes 6 to 8 servings.

BROWNIE—A rich, chocolate bar cookie, either a chewy fudge, or a light-textured cake often with a nut and fruit filling and a top layer of frosting.

Chocolate is the basic flavor for this traditionally American delight, but there are other varieties—vanilla and butterscotch (made with butterscotch chips or brown sugar). Frozen brownies are another variation with chocolate ice cream between the cookie and frosting layer.

While brownies are often made by the homemaker from chocolate or butterscotch mixes, as chewy fudge or cake, they also can be purchased from the supermarket or bakery, ready-to-eat. If in the frozen foods section of the supermarket, they are ready to eat when thawed.

Cake Brownies

These chocolate frosted, cakelike cookies go well with ice cream for dessert—

    ¼ cup butter or margarine
    1 cup sugar
    2 egg yolks
    ¼ cup milk
    ½ teaspoon vanilla
    2 1-ounce squares unsweetened
         chocolate, melted and cooled
              •   •   •
    ⅔ cup sifted all-purpose flour
    ½ teaspoon baking powder
    ½ teaspoon salt
    ⅓ cup chopped nuts
    2 stiffly beaten egg whites
         Chocolate Frosting

Cream butter and sugar till fluffy. Add egg yolks, milk, and vanilla; beat well. Stir in melted chocolate. Sift together flour, baking powder, and salt; add to creamed mixture and mix well. Stir in chopped nuts. Fold in egg whites. Turn into greased and floured 9x9x2-inch baking pan. Bake at 350° for 25 to 30 minutes. Cool. Frost. Makes 16 brownies.

Chocolate Frosting: Cream 2 tablespoons softened butter or margarine, ¼ cup chocolate-flavored malted-milk powder, and dash salt. Slowly beat in 1 cup sifted confectioners' sugar and enough light cream to make spreading consistency. Spread over cake brownies.

Fudge Brownies

Rich, chewy brownies—

> ½ cup butter or margarine
> 2 1-ounce squares unsweetened
>   chocolate
> 1 cup sugar
> 2 eggs
> 1 teaspoon vanilla
> ¾ cup sifted all-purpose flour
> ½ cup chopped walnuts

In medium saucepan melt butter and chocolate. Remove from heat; stir in sugar. Blend in eggs one at a time. Add vanilla. Stir in flour and chopped walnuts; mix well. Spread in greased 8x8x2-inch pan. Bake at 350° for 30 minutes. Cool. Cut into 16 squares.

Serve brownies for snacks or as a dessert—either alone or with fruit or ice cream. Because brownies are moist and not likely to break, they are especially good to pack for picnics, in lunchboxes, and for mailing. (See also *Cookie*.)

Butterscotch Brownies

> ¼ cup butter or margarine
> 1 cup brown sugar
> 1 egg
> ½ teaspoon vanilla
> ¾ cup sifted all-purpose flour
> ½ teaspoon salt
> ¼ teaspoon ground nutmeg
> 1 egg white
> 1 tablespoon light corn syrup
> ½ cup granulated sugar
> ½ cup chopped nuts

In saucepan combine butter and brown sugar; cook and stir over low heat till bubbly. Cool slightly. Beat in egg and vanilla. Sift together flour, salt, and nutmeg. Stir into sugar mixture. Spread in greased 8x8x2-inch pan.

Beat egg white to soft peaks; gradually add corn syrup, then sugar, a small amount at a time, beating till *very stiff peaks* form. Fold in chopped nuts. Spread over dough. Bake at 350° for 25 to 30 minutes. Cool; cut in 2-inch squares. Makes 16 squares.

Tri-Level Brownies

Bottom Layer:

> ½ cup sifted all-purpose flour
> ¼ teaspoon baking soda
> ¼ teaspoon salt
> 1 cup quick-cooking rolled oats
> ½ cup brown sugar
> 6 tablespoons butter or
>   margarine, melted

Sift flour, soda, and salt together; mix with rolled oats and brown sugar. Stir in melted butter. Pat mixture in 11x7x1½-inch baking pan; bake at 350° for 10 minutes.

Middle Layer:

> 1 1-ounce square unsweetened
>   chocolate, melted *or* 1
>   envelope no-melt unsweetened
>   chocolate
> ¼ cup butter or margarine, melted
> ¾ cup granulated sugar
> 1 egg
> ⅔ cup sifted all-purpose flour
> ¼ teaspoon baking powder
> ¼ teaspoon salt
> ¼ cup milk
> ½ teaspoon vanilla
> ½ cup chopped walnuts

Combine chocolate, butter, and sugar; add egg and beat well. Sift flour, baking powder, and salt together; add alternately with milk and vanilla to chocolate mixture. Fold in nuts.

Spread batter over baked Bottom Layer. Return to oven and bake at 350° for 25 minutes.

Top Layer:

> 1 1-ounce square unsweetened
>   chocolate
> 2 tablespoons butter or margarine
> 1½ cups sifted confectioners'
>   sugar
> 1 teaspoon vanilla

Place chocolate and butter in small saucepan. Stir over low heat till chocolate melts. Remove from heat and add confectioners' sugar and vanilla. Blend in enough hot water (about 2 tablespoons) to make almost pourable consistency. Spread over baked Middle Layer of brownies. Cut in bars. Top each with walnut half, if desired. Makes 16 large bars.

Pineapple-Chocolate Squares

    ¾ cup shortening
  1½ cups sugar
    1 teaspoon vanilla
    3 eggs
    1 cup sifted all-purpose flour
    1 teaspoon baking powder
    ½ teaspoon salt
    ½ teaspoon ground cinnamon

        • • •

    ¼ cup chopped pecans
    2 1-ounce squares unsweetened
       chocolate, melted and cooled
    1 8¾-ounce can crushed pineapple,
       well-drained (¾ cup)
    Confectioners' sugar

Cream shortening, sugar, and vanilla till fluffy; beat in eggs. Sift flour, baking powder, salt, and cinnamon together; stir into creamed mixture. Divide batter in half.

    To one half batter add nuts and chocolate. Spread in greased 9x9x2-inch baking pan. To second half add pineapple; spread *carefully* over chocolate layer. Bake at 350° for 35 minutes. Sprinkle with sifted confectioners' sugar. Cut into squares.

Brownie Treats

Mint and chocolate, a fresh flavor combination—

    1 16-ounce package brownie mix
    ½ 7-ounce jar marshmallow creme
    2 tablespoons green crème
       de menthe
    Vanilla ice cream

Prepare fudge-type brownies according to package directions. Cool slightly; cut into large bars or squares. Blend together the marshmallow creme and crème de menthe. To serve, top each brownie with a scoop of ice cream. Spoon mint sauce over top. Makes 6 servings.

Special for company or family

Brownies are a special treat any time of the day. Top off a gala evening with Tri-Level Brownies and steaming cups of coffee.

BROWN RICE—Unpolished rice. Only the outer hull and a small part of the bran are removed during processing. Brown rice has a color range of brown to yellow, nut-like flavor, and slightly chewy texture. Nutritionally, it contains minerals, the B vitamins—niacin and thiamine—and some iron. A one-half cup serving of brown rice supplies about 180 calories.

Store brown rice in a tightly covered container at room temperature. It doesn't keep as long as white rice because of the oil content in the bran. Cook this rice for 45 minutes to 1 hour with 2½ cups of liquid for each cup of raw rice. One cup uncooked rice yields three to four cups when cooked. Use brown rice in stuffings and dressings, or serve as a side dish especially with wild game. (See also *Rice*.)

BROWN SAUCE—A basic sauce, also known as "espagnole," made by browning flour in butter or margarine and adding brown stock. Brown sauce is served with meat and poultry or used as a base for making other sauces. Ingredients such as tomato purée and mushrooms combine well with the flavor of brown sauce. (See also *Sauce*.)

Brown Sauce

Use homemade stock or canned broth—

    1½ tablespoons butter or margarine
    1½ tablespoons all-purpose flour
     2 cups Brown Stock (See *Stock*)
       or 1 10½-ounce can condensed
       beef broth plus water to
       make 2 cups

Melt butter in saucepan; blend in flour. Cook and stir over low heat till browned. Stir in stock. Bring to boiling and cook 3 to 5 minutes. Reduce heat and simmer 30 minutes, stirring occasionally. Makes about 1⅓ cups.

Gourmet Sauce

Boil 2 cups Brown Sauce till reduced to half the volume. Add ⅓ cup dry white wine. Bring just to boiling. Serve hot with roast beef or veal, baked ham, or chicken. Makes 1⅓ cups.

BROWN SUGAR—Crystals of partially refined sugar which are covered with a film of dark syrup. The brown, moist sugar has a flavor resembling molasses or butterscotch. Because it is unrefined, brown sugar is richer in minerals than white sugar.

As the brown sugar is refined, its flavor becomes milder and its color changes from dark brown (similar to the color of roasted coffee) to almost white. It is marketed as "dark brown" or "light brown."

When granulated, brown sugar has less moisture and pours easily. As a guide, substitute one and one-third cups granulated brown sugar for one cup regular brown sugar in dishes which are moist.

There are a multitude of uses for brown sugar. Besides use as a sweetener for cereals, fruits, and beverages, it can be used in making breads, gingerbreads, cakes, desserts, cookies, candies, sauces, and glazes. Brown sugar used in recipes should be packed into the measuring cup.

Although this sugar is basically used in cooking, children are often caught snitching a handful to nibble. And their parents and grandparents probably have pleasant memories of how they enjoyed eating a chunk of brown sugar from the pantry when they were children.

Brown Sugar Nut Roll

    2 cups granulated sugar
    1 cup brown sugar
    1 cup evaporated milk
    ¼ cup light corn syrup
    1 cup chopped pecans

Butter sides of heavy 2-quart saucepan. In it combine sugars, milk, corn syrup, and dash salt. Stir over medium heat till sugars dissolve and mixture boils. Cook to soft ball stage (236°) stirring frequently. (Mixture will curdle while cooking, but becomes smooth when beaten.) Immediately remove from heat; cool to lukewarm (110°). *Do not* stir candy.

Beat till candy begins to hold its shape. Turn out on buttered surface. Knead till it can be shaped, keeping hands well buttered. Shape in two 7-inch rolls; roll immediately in chopped nuts, pressing to coat well. Wrap and chill. Cut in ½-inch slices. Makes about 28 pieces.

Bran Apricot Squares

½ cup dried apricots
1 cup water
½ cup butter or margarine
¼ cup granulated sugar
½ cup sifted all-purpose flour
¾ cup whole bran cereal

• • •

2 eggs
1 cup brown sugar
½ teaspoon vanilla
½ cup sifted all-purpose flour
½ teaspoon baking powder
½ teaspoon salt
½ cup chopped walnuts

Dice apricots and add water. Simmer covered 10 minutes; drain. Set aside to cool. Cream butter and granulated sugar. Stir in ½ cup flour and bran. Press over bottom of 9x9x2-inch baking pan. Bake at 350° for 15 minutes.

Meanwhile, beat eggs till thick and lemon-colored. Stir in brown sugar and vanilla. Sift together ½ cup flour, baking powder, and salt; add to egg mixture. Stir in cooked apricots and walnuts. Pour over baked bran layer. Bake at 350° for 25 to 30 minutes. Cool; cut in squares. Makes about 18 squares.

Store brown sugar in tightly covered containers, preferably in the refrigerator to avoid loss of moisture. It becomes hard if the natural moistness evaporates. But when brown sugar does become dry and hard, simply place a slice of apple or bread in the container and cover tightly to restore moisture. (See also *Sugar*.)

BRUISE—To crush or injure. On most fruits or vegetables, bruising is harmful, and is generally caused by pinching or pressing. This brings about a discolored spot and hastens spoilage. However, contrary to popular belief, the action of bruising can be beneficial to some foods. Mint leaves are an example where bruising releases the subtle flavors in the leaves.

BRUNCH—A late-morning meal. Brunch is a combination of breakfast and lunch, not only of the words, but also of the foods, and of the hours served.

Holidays and weekends are ideal times for a brunch. Serve brunch anytime between 10:00 a.m. and 1:00 p.m. This is a popular time for both the hostess and the guests. The hostess has time to prepare the food before the guests arrive—a boon to the woman who is employed outside the home and finds it difficult to entertain after being at work all day. The guests can sleep late, dress leisurely, attend church, or even engage in a sports event before the brunch. And after the meal, there is still time left in the day for other activities.

How to plan: Substantial breakfast foods fit well into a brunch menu. Begin the brunch with fresh fruits and juices, such as tomato juice or a Bloody Mary. Then follow with breads, rolls, and coffee cake, piping hot. The fragrance of baking bread fills the home and arouses the appetites of the waiting brunchers. Include butter or margarine along with an assortment of jams, jellies, and honey.

Spear Dilly-Brussels Sprouts on wooden picks for an appetizer. These tiny, cabbage-like vegetables are a perfect bite size.

But brunch need not only be based on breakfast foods. Merge breakfast with lunch. Include scrambled eggs, Canadian-style bacon, crisp strips of bacon, and waffles from the breakfast menu, then add assortments from the lunch menu—creamed chicken, sweetbreads, hot vegetables, and sliced tomatoes. However, skip the dessert.

For drinks, hot coffee, hot tea, or milk are excellent. And for many people, cocktails and champagne can also be included on the brunch beverage list.

How to serve: Greet your guests with plenty of hot coffee—a most essential and welcome eye-opener. If the appetizer is a juice, you may serve it before the main course while the guests are moving about.

Any style of service is acceptable. Buffet service works easily and fits into the informal atmosphere of the brunch. Guests serve themselves as they arrive rather than waiting for everyone to be seated. On a bright spring morning, move the buffet to the patio, or serve the buffet indoors and then let the guests carry their food on a tray to the patio. Small groups can be served family style.

BRUSH—A utensil with hair or bristles attached to a long handle. A useful addition to any kitchen. Ideal for coating breads or meats with butter or liquids, such as in basting, and for greasing muffin tins and waffle bakers. (See also *Utensil.*)

BRUSSELS SPROUTS—A delicate-flavored vegetable of the cabbage family. The heads or sprouts, which resemble cabbages but are only an inch in diameter, grow on the stalk of the plant. They are named for Brussels, Belgium, where they were first grown during the fourteenth century.

Today this plant is grown in areas with a fairly long, cool growing season like that of northern Europe. California and New York are the major producers in America.

Nutritional value: Brussels sprouts have only 36 calories in an average serving, but are rich in vitamin C and have some of the B vitamin, riboflavin. Since they are also low in sodium, Brussels sprouts are a good food for persons on a salt-free diet.

How to buy: Fresh Brussels sprouts are available primarily from September to February. The peak production being in November. When purchasing, select small to medium heads which are bright green, firm, and compact. Avoid discolored leaves; these indicate poor quality. One pound makes four servings.

How to store: Enclose sprouts in clear plastic wrap and store in the refrigerator crisper. Brussels sprouts are perishable so be sure to use them within two days.

To freeze, cut off stem, remove outer leaves, and wash. Blanch by boiling 3 to 5 minutes and then chilling in ice water 3 to 5 minutes. Seal in moisture-vaporproof bags, label, and freeze. Use within 11 months. One pound of fresh vegetables yields one pint of frozen.

How to prepare: Cut off stems and be careful not to cut too closely, or the leaves will fall off. Remove wilted or discolored leaves and wash. Cut large sprouts in half so all will cook in the same amount of time. Cook fresh or frozen Brussels sprouts covered in a small amount of boiling salted water only until tender—usually about 10 to 15 minutes for fresh, and 5 to 10 minutes for frozen. Overcooking destroys the delicate flavor of Brussels sprouts.

How to use: Brussels sprouts are used primarily as a side-dish vegetable. However, they can be used as appetizers or as ingredients in salads and casseroles.

Salt, pepper, and butter or margarine are all that's needed for Brussels sprouts to be well seasoned. However, lemon juice, cheese sauce, hollandaise, and sour cream are often added for variety. Basil leaves, caraway seed, dillweed, dry mustard, and nutmeg accent the flavor of Brussels sprouts. (See also *Vegetables.*)

Dilly-Brussels Sprouts

Cook one 10-ounce package frozen Brussels sprouts; drain. Mix ½ cup Italian salad dressing, ½ teaspoon dried dillweed, crushed, and 1 tablespoon sliced green onion. Pour over cooked sprouts; chill several hours.

Brussels Sprouts in Aspic

>4 cups tomato juice
>6 onion slices
>4 lemon slices
>Tops of 6 stalks celery, with leaves
>2 bay leaves
>2 3-ounce packages lemon-flavored gelatin
>2 teaspoons prepared horseradish
>½ teaspoon salt
>Dash pepper
>1 10-ounce package frozen Brussels sprouts, cooked and drained
>2 tablespoons Italian salad dressing

Combine tomato juice, onion, lemon, celery, and bay leaves; simmer 10 minutes. Strain. Dissolve gelatin in the hot liquid. Add horseradish, salt, and pepper. Chill till partially set. Meanwhile, quarter Brussels sprouts; toss with salad dressing. Chill. Arrange sprouts in 6½-cup ring mold; add gelatin mixture. Chill till firm, about 5 hours. Makes 10 to 12 servings.

Brussels Sprouts and Mushrooms

>1 pint fresh Brussels sprouts*
>1 teaspoon salt
>4 cups cold water
>1 cup boiling water
>1 pint fresh mushrooms, sliced
>3 tablespoons butter or margarine
>Salt
>Dash pepper
>2 tablespoons chopped canned pimiento

Wash and trim sprouts. Put in saucepan with 1 teaspoon salt and 4 cups cold water; soak 30 minutes. Drain and rinse well. Put in saucepan with 1 cup boiling water. Cook covered till just tender, about 15 minutes. Drain. Meanwhile, cook mushrooms in butter or margarine till tender and golden brown. Add to sprouts and season with salt and pepper to taste. Put in serving dish and garnish with chopped pimiento. Makes 6 servings.

*One 10-ounce package frozen Brussels sprouts may be substituted for fresh. Cook as directed on package; drain and use as above.

Blue Cheesed Sprouts

>2 10-ounce packages frozen Brussels sprouts
>½ ounce blue cheese, crumbled (2 tablespoons)
>¼ cup butter or margarine

Cook Brussels sprouts according to package directions. Drain thoroughly. Melt butter in small saucepan; blend in cheese. Toss with hot drained sprouts. Makes 6 servings.

Brussels Sprouts Polonaise

>2 pounds Brussels sprouts (about 8 cups)
>¼ cup butter or margarine
>¼ cup fine dry bread crumbs
>1 hard-cooked egg yolk, sieved
>2 tablespoons snipped parsley

Wash Brussels sprouts; cut large ones in half. Cook in small amount boiling salted water till just tender, about 12 to 15 minutes. Drain. Heat butter in small saucepan or skillet till it begins to brown; add bread crumbs, egg yolk, and snipped parsley. Spoon mixture over sprouts; toss lightly. Makes 6 to 8 servings.

Toss tender sprouts in sieved egg yolk, parsley, crumbs, and browned butter—a French method to make Brussels Sprouts Polonaise.

Brussels Sprouts Fix-Ups

• Sprinkle cooked sprouts lightly with ground nutmeg, crushed sage, or caraway.
• Toss cooked sprouts with butter or margarine and warm croutons.
• Add sliced canned water chestnuts to sprouts for added crispness.

Brussels Sprouts Soufflé

Main dish at lunch or side dish at dinner—

      ¼ cup butter or margarine
      ¼ cup all-purpose flour
      1 cup milk
      4 egg yolks
      1 cup shredded Cheddar cheese
      1 10-ounce package frozen Brussels
          sprouts, cooked, drained, and
          finely chopped (about 2 cups)
      4 egg whites

Melt butter in saucepan; blend in flour and ½ teaspoon salt. Add milk all at once; cook and stir till mixture thickens and bubbles. Beat egg yolks till thick and lemon-colored. Blend some of the hot mixture into egg yolks; return to hot mixture and stir rapidly.

Stir cheese and finely chopped sprouts into sauce. Remove pan from heat. Beat egg whites until stiff but not dry; fold whites into hot mixture. Turn into an *ungreased* 2-quart soufflé dish. Bake at 350° till knife inserted off-center comes out clean, about 40 minutes. Serve immediately. Makes 4 to 6 servings.

BRUT *(broot)*—Very dry. A term used to describe wines and meaning the opposite of sweet. (See *Champagne, Wines and Spirits* for additional information.)

BUCKWHEAT—A plant that produces triangular seeds which are made into flour and cereal. The flour is frequently used in making pancakes, called buckwheat cakes.

Originally grown in China, this plant thrives in poor to medium-rich soil. American pioneers used buckwheat as a staple food because it grew quickly and was easy to mill. Therefore, many of the authentic American recipes use buckwheat.

Today, Pennsylvania and New York are the major producers of the buckwheat used in America. Wheat flours are usually mixed with the dark, pungent buckwheat to tame the strong taste before being put on the market. Buckwheat flour is sold in two forms—dark and light—depending on the amount of wheat flour added to the buckwheat. Both types contain potassium, phosphorus, iron, and the B vitamins—thiamine and riboflavin; but the dark flour has about twice as much as the light.

Breads and griddle cakes—also called buckwheat cakes—are made from buckwheat flour. When baking with this flour, do not sift. Rather, stir the flour gently. Then, spoon it lightly into the dry measuring cup and level off with the straight edge of a knife or a spatula. (See also *Flour.*)

Buckwheat Griddle Cakes

Combine 3 cups stirred buckwheat flour, 1 cup sifted all-purpose flour, and 1 teaspoon salt. Soften 1 package active dry yeast in ¼ cup warm water (110°). Dissolve 1 teaspoon granulated sugar in 3¾ cups lukewarm water. Add yeast and stir into dry ingredients. Mix well. Cover; let stand overnight at room temperature (bowl *must not* be over half full).

The next morning stir batter. Add 2 tablespoons brown sugar, ¾ teaspoon baking soda, and 1 tablespoon salad oil. Refrigerate 1 cup batter for starter (keeps several weeks). Bake remaining batter on hot, lightly greased griddle. Makes 20 pancakes.

To use starter: Add 1 cup lukewarm water, ½ cup stirred buckwheat flour, and ½ cup sifted all-purpose flour; stir smooth. Let stand overnight as before. When ready to bake, add ½ teaspoon salt, ½ teaspoon baking soda, 2 tablespoons brown sugar, and 1 tablespoon salad oil. Again, reserve 1 cup batter for starter. Bake remaining batter as before.

BUFFALOFISH—A freshwater fish living in the Great Lakes area and in the Mississippi Valley. It belongs to the sucker family. There are three varieties of buffalofish—common, round, and smallmouth. The lean, firm flesh can be baked, fried, smoked, or boiled. (See also *Fish.*)

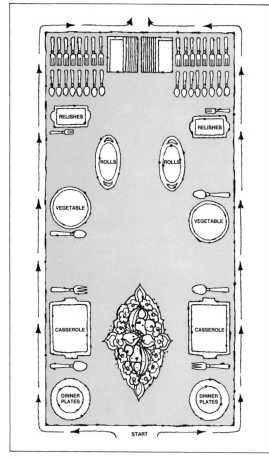

For faster and smoother serving of a large group, make twin arrangements on each side of the table so guests can form two lines.

BUFFET—An informal meal where people serve themselves food from a sideboard or table and eat either standing or sitting. These help-yourself meals take their name from the sideboard, known as a buffet, on which the meal was originally set.

It is an easy meal for the hostess to manage and still have time to enjoy the party. Buffet serving is a natural when guests outnumber the places at the dining table. Set up card tables or let guests eat lap-style from snack trays.

Plan food that can be eaten easily with forks and spoons. Avoid foods that need a knife for cutting, unless you can make room at a table for your guests. If small tables are used, silver, napkins, and cups

or glasses can be placed on the tables before guests arrive. This way, guests need only to pick up food.

If you use trays, preset them with silver and napkins. If no trays or tables are available for a large group, plates can be held on the lap. In this case, if at all possible, have some place for guests to set their beverages while they are eating.

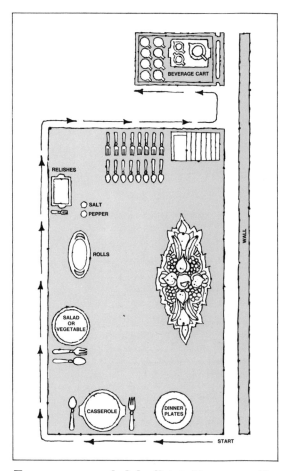

For an uncrowded buffet table, serve the beverage from a nearby cart or small table. Guests can then pick up the beverage last.

Buffet entertaining for company

Serve chicken with curried rice, crisp vegetable relishes, broccoli with lemon butter, rolls, and chiffon pie for dessert.

One main dish in a buffet menu is sufficient, although several may be offered. Just be sure that there is plenty of each, since it's likely most of your guests will want to taste each dish. If the guest list is large, make two or three casseroles as needed so there is a hot one ready to replace a dish that's emptied. Also, have a second bowl of salad in the refrigerator to replace the salad on the table when it begins to look a little wilted. Expect guests to go back for seconds. Allow for this and you won't be caught short.

When setting up the buffet table, place it in the middle of the room so guests can circulate around it. Or, place the table just far enough away from the wall so the hostess can work easily behind it.

There are no set rules for placement of items on a buffet table but it is important that guests serve themselves in a logical sequence. Some hostesses prefer to start with the dinner plates, followed by the main dish. Next come other foods such as salad, vegetable, buttered rolls, and relishes along with serving pieces for each. Other hostesses prefer to end with the main dish. Place items near the edge of the table within easy reach. However, leave enough room near each serving dish for guests to set their plates down so they can serve themselves. Set extras, such as sauces, near the foods they accompany.

If the table is crowded, serve the beverage from a nearby cart. But if there is room on the buffet table, the beverage is the last item to be taken.

Arrange silver and napkins in neat rows so that they can be picked up just before the beverage. Of course, for a sit-down buffet, the napkins and silver, possibly the beverage cups, along with the cream and sugar are set at small tables. In this case, the beverage can be served after the guests have their food and are seated.

After guests have finished the main course, the plates should be collected by the hostess and any helpers as unobtrusively as possible. The dessert is then brought out and served to each person with the dessert silver. Or, each guest can go back to the buffet table which has been cleared and reset, or to a side table, where he can serve himself. (See also *Table Setting*.)

BUGLOSS *(byoo' glos, -glôs)*—A plant bearing blue flowers. The fresh flowers are used in salads, the dried flowers as an herb, and the leaves as a vegetable. Some say that a favorite salad of Louis XIII included bugloss.

BULGUR *(bul gur', bul'-)*—A form of wheat considered a basic food in some Middle Eastern countries. It is now processed in the United States by cleaning and washing, cooking, drying, partially debranning, coarsely cracking, and then sifting.

Bulgar is high in the B vitamins, niacin, riboflavin, and thiamine and is also high in protein. It contains about 85 calories per ½ cup cooked wheat.

When cooked, the wheat becomes tender but retains the shape of the kernel pieces, giving the cooked bulgur a chewy texture. It is used as an extender in soups, meat dishes, and casseroles. Sometimes it's sold as wheat pilaf. (See also *Wheat*.)

BULLHEAD—A name for several members of the catfish family found in fresh waters of North America. (See also *Catfish*.)

BUN—Individual breads, usually prepared with yeast, that are molded or baked in muffin pans. They can be small, round, sweetened or unsweetened rolls eaten with coffee for breakfast, such as hot cross buns. They may contain raisins, candied fruits, or nuts and be covered with an icing. The name is also given to the round soft roll eaten with hamburgers and the long narrow roll eaten with frankfurters.

Swedish Lucia Buns

　　2 **packages active dry yeast**
　　5 **to 5½ cups sifted all-purpose
　　　　flour**
　1½ **cups milk**
　　½ **cup sugar**
　　½ **cup butter or margarine**
　1½ **teaspoons salt**
　　　Dash powdered saffron
　　3 **beaten eggs**
　　1 **slightly beaten egg**
　　　Raisins
　　　Sugar

In large mixing bowl combine yeast and *3 cups* flour. In saucepan heat milk, sugar, butter, salt, and saffron just till warm, stirring occasionally to melt butter. Add to dry mixture in mixing bowl. Add the 3 eggs. Beat at low speed with electric mixer for ½ minute, scraping sides of bowl constantly. Beat 3 minutes at high speed. By hand, stir in enough of remaining flour to make a soft dough. Turn out onto lightly floured surface. Knead till smooth. Place in a greased bowl, turning once to grease surface. Cover; let rise in a warm place till double, about 1½ hours.

Divide dough into 24 pieces. Roll each piece into a rope about 12 inches long. Cut in half. Form each half into an S-shape, curving ends. Cross two of these, forming an X with coiled ends. Brush buns with the remaining egg. Place a raisin in center of each coil and one in center of roll. Sprinkle lightly with a little sugar. Place on greased baking sheet. Let rise in warm place till nearly double, about 1 hour. Bake at 375° till the buns are lightly browned, 15 to 20 minutes. Makes 24 buns.

BUNDENFLEISCH—Air-dried beef from the Swiss Alps. Bindenfleisch is an alternate spelling. (See also *Bindenfleisch*.)

BURBOT *(bûr′ buht)*—A fish living in the fresh waters of northern United States and Canada. It is related to the cod.

BURGOO *(bûr′ g$\overline{oo}$)*—A regional name, mostly in the South, for a thick meat and vegetable soup or stew. The name is also applied to some types of oatmeal porridge.

Swedish Lucia Buns make a delightful Christmas gift when presented in an attractive napkin-lined basket. Type the recipe on a card and present it along with the freshly baked buns.

BURGUNDY—1. One of the most famous grape-growing regions in France producing various types of wine—from dry white wines to full-bodied, robust red wines. 2. The name given to red and white table wines of this type.

The story of Burgundy wines dates back many centuries. Some attribute the planting of vines in Burgundy to Charlemagne, while others suggest that Italian vines were planted during Caesar's conquest of Gaul. During this period, feudal lords gave vineyards to the church, possibly thinking they would be rewarded in heaven. Under the care of the monks, the lands of Burgundy grew and prospered.

During the French Revolution, the state took over many of the vineyards and sold them to the people. As a result, vineyards were owned by a number of proprietors. Today, this is still a distinctive factor of the vineyards of Burgundy, in contrast to those of Bordeaux where most vineyards are owned by an individual proprietor.

In America, the explorers and colonists found wild grapes growing when they landed, but these vines were different from the European varieties. Around the mid-1800s, cuttings and wine-making traditions were brought from Europe. Vines imported from Burgundy included the Pinot Noir and Gamay grapes used for red wines, and the Pinot Blanc and Pinot Chardonnay used for white wines. These traditional European vines seemed to grow best in the mild California climate.

Many of the American-produced Burgundy wines have varietal names. These are given when wines are named after the principal variety of grape used in their production. For example, some American red Burgundies are called Pinot Noir or Gamay, and white Burgundies are called Chardonnay, Pinot Chardonnay, and Pinot Blanc. To be given these names in the United States, however, the wines must derive at least 51 percent of their volume from the grape after which they are named.

When the label on the bottle reads California Burgundy, the wine has merely been named generically, meaning that it was produced in California from a blend of grapes but possesses similar characteristics to European wines of the same name.

How Burgundy is produced: Wine in Burgundy is made similarly to wines of other areas of France. However, the top-quality wines from this region are normally made from one grape, whereas wines from the Bordeaux region are usually a blend of several grapes. When making Burgundies, sugar is sometimes added to stabilize the vintage, especially in poor grape growing years, while Bordeaux wines are generally prepared without added sugar. Because the vineyards of Burgundy are small and operated by many owners, the wines are often made in private cellars and are called "estate bottled." Wines of Burgundy mature quicker than those of Bordeaux.

Burgundy wines are bottled in distinctively shaped containers. For red wines, a stout, dark green bottle with sloping shoulders is used; and for white French Burgundies, similar light-colored bottles.

Kinds of Burgundy: The names on the bottles of French wines are carefully controlled. The name can be that of the district, commune, village, or vineyard. Usually the more specific the name, the better the wine. Ordinary wines bear the generic name of the region, while the very best wines are named after great vineyards.

French Burgundy wines are made in four regions: the area around Chablis in Yonne; the Côte d'Or; the Mâconnais; and the Côte Chalonnaise.

Many of the best Burgundies come from the Côte d'Or area. This area is divided into two sections—Côte de Nuits, known for its red wines, and Côte de Beaune, known principally for its white wines. Among the red wines of the Côte de Nuits are Chambertin, Romanée-Conti, and Musigny. Fine white wines of the Côte de Beaune are Montrachet and Meursault. All of these are named after vineyards, except Meursault, the name of a commune.

From the Mâconnais and Beaujolais area comes the red Beaujolais wine which has a fruity aroma, and the pale white Pouilly-Fuissé. Chablis, from the Yonne region, is one of the driest white wines.

Sparkling Burgundies made from white, red, or rosé still wines are produced in France and America. They are sweeter and more full-bodied than Champagne.

How to store: Burgundy wines should be kept in a cool, dark place and those with corks should be placed on their sides so that the cork doesn't dry out. If the cork dries out, it shrinks from the sides of the bottle and lets in air which can weaken or spoil the wine. Another fact to keep in mind is that Burgundy, like other wines, should be kept from excessive vibration.

If the bottle is opened and the contents not entirely used, the remaining wine should be transferred to a smaller bottle so that some of the air will be excluded. Then the bottle should be tightly corked. If you are planning to use only a small quantity of a wine for cooking, it's best to only buy a half-bottle of wine.

How to use: Burgundy can be used as a beverage and in cooking. Used in the preparation of meat dishes, it gives a particularly delightful flavor.

In cooking, the flavor of the wine is meant to be subtle and to enhance the natural flavor of the food. When wine is heated, the alcohol evaporates and leaves only the distinctive Burgundy flavor.

As a beverage, red Burgundy is a robust, full-bodied, dry table wine and is especially good with beef, game, and cheese. The white Burgundies, since they are light and delicate in flavor, go best with seafood and poultry. However, keep in mind that these are just guidelines; taste preference should be the deciding factor when choosing wines.

One of the most popular main dishes prepared with wine is Beef Burgundy. This company special main dish is served over rice or noodles. Accompany with a robust red Burgundy wine.

Serve red Burgundies at a cool room temperature, not chilled. Serve white Burgundies cold, especially in hot weather. However, don't over-chill the wine. One or two hours in the refrigerator or about 30 minutes in an ice bucket is sufficient.

When serving Burgundies, uncork red wines an hour or two before serving. This allows the wine to "breathe." White wines and Beaujolais can usually be uncorked just before serving. Pour into clear, stemmed, preferably tulip-shaped wine glasses. The uncolored glass allows the true color and clarity of the wine to show through while the tulip shape concentrates the bouquet. Glasses should be large enough so that they need only be filled half full. (See also *Wines and Spirits*.)

Beef Burgundy

2 pounds beef round steak, ¼-inch thick
3 tablespoons all-purpose flour
3 tablespoons butter or margarine
⅓ cup chopped onion
1 tablespoon snipped parsley
1 clove garlic, crushed
1 medium bay leaf
¾ teaspoon salt
Dash pepper
1 6-ounce can whole mushrooms, drained
¾ cup red Burgundy
¾ cup water
Cooked rice or noodles

Cut round steak into bite-size cubes; shake with the flour to coat evenly, being sure all the flour is used. Melt butter or margarine in large skillet. Brown part of the steak cubes on all sides; remove from skillet and repeat with remaining meat pieces. Return all the meat to the skillet; remove skillet from heat.

Add onion, parsley, garlic, bay leaf, salt, and pepper. Stir in the mushrooms, Burgundy, and water. Bring mixture to boiling. Reduce heat and simmer, covered, till meat is tender, about 1 hour. Remove bay leaf.

Serve over fluffy hot cooked rice or buttered cooked noodles. If desired, for buffet service transfer meat mixture to chafing dish to keep hot. Makes 6 servings.

Cranberry-Burgundy Glazed Ham

Place 1 bone-in fully-cooked ham (about 10 to 14 pounds), fat side up, in shallow roasting pan. Score fat in a diamond pattern; stud with whole cloves. Insert meat thermometer into ham. Roast meat at 325° till meat thermometer registers 130°, about 2½ to 3 hours.

Meanwhile, in saucepan stir together one 16-ounce can whole cranberry sauce, 1 cup brown sugar, ½ cup red Burgundy, and 2 teaspoons prepared mustard. Simmer the mixture, uncovered, for 5 minutes.

During the last 30 minutes of roasting time for ham, spoon half of the cranberry glaze over ham. Pass the remaining glaze as a sauce. Makes 2⅔ cups sauce.

BURNET *(bûr' nit)*—An herb belonging to the rose family, also called salad burnet. This herb is native to Europe and Asia. While it is often cultivated in kitchen gardens, it can also be found growing wild.

The leaves are deeply serrated and have a slight cucumber taste. The young leaves are best for eating, as the older ones become tough and slightly bitter.

Because of its pleasant appearance, burnet is often used as a decoration on platters and in punches. It is also used with fish salads, green salads, and sometimes in the making of homemade vinegar, to which it gives a very delicate cucumber flavor. (See also *Herb*.)

BURNT SUGAR—One of the names for caramelized sugar. It is made by heating granulated sugar in a skillet until it melts and takes on a golden brown color. This burnt sugar can be dissolved in water and used as a syrup that gives flavor to cakes, puddings, confections, and frostings. However, the more the granulated sugar is caramelized, the less sweetening power it has. (See also *Sugar*.)

A special cake for a special day

Old-fashioned Burnt-Sugar Syrup gives a→ sweet-bitter flavor and golden color to both Burnt-Sugar Cake and Frosting.

Burnt-Sugar Syrup

Melt (caramelize) ⅔ cup granulated sugar in large, heavy skillet, stirring constantly. When a deep golden brown syrup, remove from heat. Slowly add ⅔ cup boiling water. Heat and stir till all dissolves. Boil to reduce syrup to ½ cup. Set aside to cool. This is enough syrup for both Burnt-Sugar Cake and Burnt-Sugar Frosting. *Or*, half the recipe may be prepared in a small heavy saucepan. This makes enough syrup for Burnt-Sugar Frosting only.

Burnt-Sugar Cake

A tawny-colored cake—

　½ cup shortening
　1½ cups sugar
　1 teaspoon vanilla
　2 eggs
　　　• • •
　2½ cups sifted cake flour
　3 teaspoons baking powder
　½ teaspoon salt
　¾ cup cold water
　3 tablespoons Burnt-Sugar Syrup
　　　• • •
　Date Filling
　Burnt-Sugar Frosting
　Broken walnuts

Cream shortening and sugar till light. Add vanilla, then eggs, one at a time, beating 1 minute after each. Sift together flour, baking powder, and salt; add to creamed mixture alternately with water, beating smooth after each addition. Add sugar syrup. Beat thoroughly, 4 minutes at medium speed on electric mixer.

Bake in 2 greased and lightly floured 9x1½-inch round cake pans at 375° till done, about 20 minutes. (Or bake in two 8x1½-inch round pans at 350° for 25 to 30 minutes.) Cool 10 minutes; remove from pans. Cool. Fill with Date Filling and frost with Burnt-Sugar Frosting. Press broken walnuts on cake sides.

Date Filling: Combine 1½ cups pitted dates, cut up; 1 cup water; ⅓ cup sugar; and ¼ teaspoon salt in saucepan. Bring to boiling. Cook and stir over low heat till thick, about 4 minutes. Remove from heat; cool to room temperature. Fold in ¼ cup Burnt-Sugar Frosting and ¼ cup chopped walnuts.

Burnt-Sugar Frosting

　2 unbeaten egg whites
　1¼ cups granulated sugar
　¼ cup cold water
　3 to 4 tablespoons Burnt-Sugar
　　Syrup
　Dash salt
　　　• • •
　1 teaspoon vanilla

Combine egg whites, sugar, water, Burnt-Sugar Syrup, and salt in top of double boiler (not over heat). Beat ½ minute with electric or rotary beater. Place over, but not touching, boiling water and cook, beating constantly, till frosting forms stiff peaks, about 7 minutes (don't overcook).

Remove from boiling water. Pour into mixing bowl if desired. Add vanilla and beat till of spreading consistency, about 2 minutes. Frosts tops and sides of two 8- or 9-inch layers, top of 13x9-inch cake, or 24 cupcakes.

BUTTER—1. The churned, solidified fat of milk that is used in food preparation and as a spread. 2. To spread anything with the product called butter.

No one knows exactly when butter was first discovered. Legend has it that the earliest butter was discovered accidentally one day as a Middle Eastern nomad on an extended journey carried a goatskin of milk with him. As he attempted to use the milk, he found that a yellow fat had formed, due to the constant motion during travel. Discovery, whatever it really was, eventually led to primitive butter churning methods, one of which included dragging a skinful of cream behind galloping horses.

Butter is mentioned as early as Genesis in the *Holy Bible*, so it has been known for many hundreds of years.

In North America, butter was unheard of until European settlers arrived with their cattle. These animals were used not only for milk, but for the products made from milk and for food. As the number of cattle increased over the years, more butter was produced than the farm-families could consume. Consequently, this hand-churned farm-made butter was sold or traded for other necessities.

It was not until around 1870 that commercially made butter was available in the United States. One of the first steps in early production methods used by commercial creameries involved the process of letting the milk stand till it separated. But with the invention of the mechanical separator, creameries could buy the cream already separated, ready for butter making. By 1910, about 60 percent of the butter in America was commercially made.

How butter is produced: The first step in butter making is to separate the cream from the milk. The cream is then pasteurized, cooled, and held around 40° for several hours. During this time, the fat solidifies. At this point the fat is ready to be churned and the fat gathers into pea-size granules. The next step is to wash the granules and add salt and color. This mixture is worked until the salt, color, and water are uniformly distributed. One of the final steps in the production of butter is the packing operation.

It is at this point that butter is graded. This is a voluntary step in the production of butter and individual creameries pay for the service. A sample of the butter is examined closely by federal inspectors for flavor, evenness of color, and body and texture characteristics. All of these tests affect the final grade that will ultimately appear on the butter label.

The United States Department of Agriculture has set up various classifications that are commonly used. The shield can bear the letters AA, A, or B. Grade AA has a very pleasant aroma; sweet flavor; smooth, creamy texture; and the salt is completely dissolved, and well blended. Grade A butter has a pleasant flavor and rates high in quality, although it is second best. These are the two grades most generally seen in grocery stores. Grade B is butter made from selected sour cream. It is an acceptable product although it does not quite measure up to the high qualities of the top two grades.

A numerical score is also seen on some butter cartons. It is based on an official dairy industry scorecard. The butter that is marked U.S. 93 Score is equivalent to Grade AA; U.S. 92 Score is equivalent to

Grade A; U.S. 90 Score is equivalent to Grade B butter. Any butter that scores less than 90 is not considered desirable for table use. If the grade or score does not contain the prefix U.S., the butter has not been graded under federal supervision.

Nutritional value: According to United States standards, butter must contain at least 80 percent milk fat. And since fat is very important in the diet, butter is probably one of the best sources. Not only is fat a concentrated source of energy, but it is

For butter pats, fold strip of waxed paper over knife. Press down on butter stick with heavy stroke. Trim butter with parsley.

Serve butter attractively. A quick idea is to prepare Butter Roses ahead of time. The topknot of color is a tiny parsley sprig.

also digested slowly, meaning that it will give you a satisfied or full feeling for a longer period of time.

One tablespoon butter adds 100 calories to the diet. It is an excellent source of vitamin A. Summer butter will be richer in vitamin A, however, because cows have more green feed during summer months.

Kinds of butter: Butter made from sweet cream and usually lightly salted is referred to as "sweet cream butter." It is packaged in a one-pound carton containing four wrapped quarters, or in a one-pound wax paper-wrapped block. Some wrappers are marked with measurements, making them handy for cooking and baking.

You can also purchase butter that is unsalted. This butter is generally referred to in the United States as "sweet butter" and is preferred by many Europeans. Some grocery stores and supermarkets keep it in the frozen food counter.

Whipped butter is made of standard butter with air or other gases whipped into it. This results in a product that is easier to spread. A point to keep in mind, is that because part of the volume is air, whipped butter cannot be successfully substituted directly for regular butter in most instances. In the grocery store you'll find whipped butter sold in round tubs or in sticks, six to the pound.

How to store: Butter will hold its quality if properly handled and stored. It should be kept refrigerated or frozen and protected from light in order to prevent chemical changes and undesirable flavor changes.

Since butter absorbs odors and tastes from other foods rather easily, distorting its own flavor, keep butter well covered in the refrigerator. A hint to remember—butter will keep better in its own carton than just in its paper wrapper.

If butter is not to be used within the week, store it in the freezer where it will keep several months. Be sure to wrap tightly and seal for best flavor results.

How to use: Butter has many uses, one of which is as a spread. When blended with other ingredients, such as citrus peels or herbs, it adds flavor to other foods. Next

Orange-Honey Butter is delightful when served on pancakes. For a special treat, fill hot pancakes with orange marmalade.

time you're planning French toast or pancakes for brunch, serve a flavored butter. Or, for dinner, herb-seasoned butter can perk up everyday vegetable dishes.

Orange-Honey Butter

½ cup butter, softened
¼ cup honey
½ teaspoon grated orange peel

With electric mixer beat together butter, honey, and orange peel till fluffy. Garnish with additional grated orange peel. Serve with pancakes, waffles or French toast.

Herb Butter

½ cup butter, softened
½ teaspoon dried rosemary leaves, crushed
½ teaspoon dried marjoram leaves, crushed

Combine butter and herbs. Blend till light and fluffy. Serve with corn on the cob.

Zippy Butter

    ½ cup butter, softened
    1 tablespoon prepared mustard
    1 teaspoon prepared horseradish
    ½ teaspoon salt
      Dash freshly ground pepper

In a bowl combine butter, mustard, horseradish, salt, and pepper. Blend with spoon till fluffy. Serve with corn on the cob.

Caper Butter

Place ½ cup softened butter and 3 tablespoons capers *with liquid* in small mixing bowl. Beat till light and fluffy. Serve with fish.

Garlic Butter

In a bowl combine ½ cup softened butter and 1 or 2 cloves garlic, minced. Spread on slices of French bread before heating in oven or melt butter atop broiled steaks.

Lemon Butter

Melt ¼ cup butter. Add 1 tablespoon lemon juice, 1 tablespoon snipped parsley, and dash pepper. Serve with cooked asparagus, artichokes, broccoli, or fish.

Butter can be served as drawn butter, clarified butter, or it can be molded in special wooden butter molds. To make molded butter, press firm butter into specially designed butter molds. Turn out and chill till serving time.

Or, individualize the servings of butter and present it in shapes, such as *Butter Roses:* Cut stick of butter into 1-inch-thick pieces. Soften slightly, then place forefinger on top of cube. Press tines of a chilled fork at each corner parallel with tabletop and press inward; then press upward, forming petals. Top each with a parsley sprig. Chill before serving.

As an ingredient, butter adds a distinctive flavor to many items, such as cakes and cookies. (See also *Fats and Oils.*)

BUTTER *(fruit)*—A smooth-textured fruit spread that is generally less sweet than jams or jellies. It is made by cooking sieved or puréed fruit until it is very thick in consistency and almost transparent.

One of the most familiar is spicy apple butter. Bananas also make a delicious butter. (See also *Jelly.*)

Banana Butter

    2¾ pounds ripe bananas (5 large)
     ¼ cup lemon juice
     ¼ cup finely chopped maraschino
        cherries
    6½ cups sugar
     1 6-ounce bottle liquid fruit
        pectin

Mash bananas (need 3 cups). In saucepan combine mashed banana, lemon juice, maraschino cherries, and sugar. Mix well. Bring to a *full rolling boil and boil hard 1 minute*, stirring constantly. Remove from heat. Quickly stir in pectin. Skim off foam. Ladle fruit butter into hot scalded half-pint jars. Seal at once. Label jars. Makes seven ½-pint jars.

What could make a more delicious pair for a midmorning snack with coffee or tea than piping hot toast and colorful Banana Butter.

Gourmet-looking butter balls are a snap to make with the right equipment on hand and with butter at the correct temperature.

BUTTER BALL — Individual portions of chilled butter molded into balls. The trick of making butter balls is not difficult to master. Be sure the butter is firm, but not too cold. Scald two butter paddles in boiling water, then chill in ice water.

Cut butter sticks into ½-inch pats and form into the shape of a ball with fingers. Put on scored side of paddle. Holding bottom paddle still, move top paddle in circular motion with light pressure. If butter clings to paddles, scald and chill the paddles again. Put balls in ice water or on a plate and refrigerate till served.

BUTTER CAKE — A type of shortened cake made with butter as the fat. The butter gives a very distinctive and delicious flavor and aroma to the baked product. Sometimes the name is given to all cakes that are made with shortening. (See also *Cake*.)

BUTTER COOKIE — The name given to a rich cookie that usually has a high butter content and a predominant butter flavor. It's also the name given to varieties of cookies made with a cookie press, such as Swedish spritz cookies. (See also *Cookie*.)

Lemonade Cookies

Flavor comes from lemonade concentrate—

1 cup butter
1 cup sugar
2 eggs
3 cups sifted all-purpose flour
1 teaspoon baking soda
1 6-ounce can frozen lemonade
     concentrate, thawed
Sugar

Cream together butter and 1 cup sugar. Add eggs; beat till light and fluffy. Sift together flour and baking soda; add alternately to the creamed mixture with ½ *cup* of the lemonade concentrate. Drop dough from a teaspoon 2 inches apart onto *ungreased* cookie sheet.

Bake cookies at 400° till lightly browned around the edges, about 8 minutes. Brush hot cookies lightly with remaining lemonade concentrate; sprinkle with sugar. Remove cookies to cooling rack. Makes about 48 small cookies.

Keep the cookie jar filled with rich and buttery Lemonade Cookies for spur-of-the-moment snacks. Try them with ice cream.

Nut-Edged Butter Slices

A delicate butter cookie—

- 1½ cups sifted all-purpose flour
- 2 teaspoons baking powder
- ½ teaspoon salt
- ½ cup butter
- ⅔ cup sugar
- 1 egg yolk
- 2 tablespoons light cream
- 1 teaspoon vanilla
- ½ cup toasted almonds, finely chopped
- 3 tablespoons sugar
- 1 slightly beaten egg white

Sift together flour, baking powder, and salt. Cream butter and ⅔ cup sugar. Add egg yolk, cream, and vanilla; beat well. Add flour mixture gradually, beating well.

Shape dough on waxed paper into a 12x1½-inch roll. Chill 1 hour. Combine almonds and 3 tablespoons sugar. Brush dough with egg white.

Serve butter attractively in the form of butter curls. Have hot water handy to dip butter curler into after making each curl.

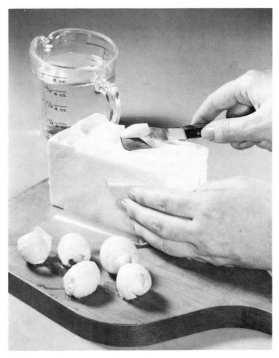

Roll in almond-sugar mixture, pressing nuts in firmly. Cut in ¼-inch slices. Place on lightly greased cookie sheet. Bake at 400° till cookies are done, 7 to 10 minutes. Makes 48.

BUTTERCUP SQUASH — A small, hard-shell, dark green winter squash that is round in shape with a rough surface. It is known as a turban squash.

After purchase, the squash should be stored in a cool, dark place. Buttercup squash is generally peeled and cut up before it is baked or steamed. The cooked vegetable resembles a sweet potato in both flavor and color. (See also *Squash*.)

BUTTER CURL — An attractive form for individual butter portions. To make butter curls, dip a butter curler in hot water, then draw gadget lengthwise down a stick or block of chilled butter, making curls about ⅛ inch thick. The butter should be firm, but not too cold or hard. Then, repeat, dipping curler in hot water before making each curl. Keep butter curls chilled in the refrigerator until serving time.

BUTTERFAT — A term long associated with the fat content of milk but more correctly called milk fat. In homogenized milk, the milk fat is broken up into small particles and then is dispersed permanently in the milk. In most states, whole milk must contain at least 3.25 percent milk fat while skim milk and buttermilk must contain less than 0.1 percent milk fat. The fat improves the palatability and flavor of milk.

By law, butter must contain at least 80 percent milk fat. Different creams have varying amounts of milk fat: light cream— 18 percent; half and half—10 to 12 percent; and whipping cream—30 to 36 percent milk fat.

BUTTERFISH — A small flatfish weighing up to one-half pound and measuring up to 12 inches long. The meat is oily, texture is soft, and flavor is good. It can be baked, fried, broiled, or panbroiled and served with a sauce. A member of the mackerel family, it is found off the eastern coast of the United States. Other names for this fish are gunnel or dollarfish.

BUTTERFLY CUT—A meat-cutting technique in which a boned or boneless cut of meat or seafood is split almost all the way through the center, then spread open flat. The meat has an attractive butterfly shape with twice the cut surface exposed. Besides greater eye appeal, the butterfly cut cooks more quickly.

At the meat counter the shopper may find butterfly cut pork chops and thick slices of pork or beef tenderloin among the prepackaged meats. Smoked pork chops are sometimes marketed this way, too. A boned leg of lamb is another meat for butterfly cutting but may require a special order. With practice and a sharp knife, most meats can be butterfly cut at home.

Shrimp is one of the most delightful examples of this preparation method. The shelled, deveined shrimp are butterflied by slitting along the back, then flattening. If desired, a slit can be made in the back portion of the shrimp and the tail pulled through. Lobster tails make especially handsome servings when butterfly cut. A butterfly cut can be used when filleting fish if a flap of underbody skin is left attached to the fillets.

Partially thaw frozen tails. Cut through center of hard top shell and meat but not through undershell membrane. Spread open.

Butterfly pork chops make handsome meaty servings because twice as much of the meat shows. An herb-crumb mixture coats these chops and emphasizes the butterfly shape. After browning in an oven-going skillet, the meat is baked until fork tender.

Thick-cut pork loin and rib chops are excellent choices for butterfly cutting. First the bone is removed from the chop and the large muscle is split almost all the way through the center, then meat is spread open flat to resemble butterfly wings.

The "winged" cuts of meat and seafood are cooked in the same way that the original cut would be: shrimp are batter-dipped and deep-fat fried or baked in a special sauce, and lobster and tender steaks or chops are broiled or panfried. Often an herb rub or seasoned coating is applied.

Butterfly Pork Chops

    **4 rib or loin pork chops,
       butterflied**

        • • •

**½ cup fine dry bread crumbs
1 teaspoon salt
¼ teaspoon dried marjoram leaves,
    ground
   Dash pepper
1 beaten egg**

Trim fat from chops. Heat fat in oven-going skillet till 2 tablespoons melted fat have collected; remove trimmings. Combine crumbs, salt, marjoram, and pepper. Dip chops in egg, then in crumb mixture. Slowly brown chops in hot fat. Bake, covered, at 350° about 60 minutes or till chops are fork-tender. Serves 4.

BUTTERMILK—1. The liquid remaining after butter is churned. 2. A cultured-milk product. Both types of buttermilk are smooth, fairly thick, and have a distinctive, slightly sour and tangy flavor.

The buttermilk in general distribution in the United States is made with a specially-prepared bacterial culture which is added to fresh skim milk, and allowed to ferment under carefully controlled conditions. In some parts of the country butter granules are added to cultured buttermilk to increase the resemblance between it and natural buttermilk.

Nutritional value: Because of the low milk-fat content, buttermilk—both natural and cultured—is high in nutritive value and low in calories. As such, it is a boon to the weight watchers. One cup contains 80 calories. Buttermilk is high in protein, calcium, phosphorus, and potassium. Since salt is often added to accentuate buttermilk's flavor, sodium is also present.

How to use buttermilk: Although its popularity as a beverage is not widespread, the distinctive flavor of buttermilk is enjoyed in a variety of dishes. Perhaps the best known are buttermilk biscuits and buttermilk pancakes. The pleasing tang makes it useful also in chilled soups and custards. It gives a delicious flavor and texture to cakes, cookies, and breads.

When buttermilk is used in batters and doughs, baking soda in the proportion of ½ teaspoon to 1 cup of buttermilk is usually added. This reduces the acidity and provides some leavening. (See also *Milk.*)

Buttermilk Pancakes

**1¼ cups sifted all-purpose flour
  1 tablespoon sugar
  2 teaspoons baking powder
  ½ teaspoon baking soda
  ½ teaspoon salt
  1 beaten egg
  1 cup buttermilk
  2 tablespoons salad oil**

Sift together dry ingredients. Combine egg, buttermilk, and salad oil; add to dry ingredients, stirring just till moistened. Bake on hot greased griddle. Makes eight 4-inch pancakes.

Buttermilk White Cake

**2¼ cups sifted cake flour
1½ cups sugar
  1 teaspoon salt
  1 teaspoon baking soda
  1 teaspoon baking powder
  ¼ cup butter or margarine
  ¼ cup shortening
1½ teaspoons vanilla
  1 cup buttermilk
  4 egg whites**

Sift dry ingredients into mixing bowl. Add butter, shortening, vanilla, and ¾ *cup* of the buttermilk; beat 2 minutes at medium speed on electric mixer. Add remaining buttermilk and egg whites. Beat 2 minutes. Bake in 2 greased and floured 9x1½-inch round pans at 350° for 25 to 30 minutes. Cool 10 minutes; remove from pans. Cool. Frost, if desired.

Chilled Cuke-Buttermilk Soup is a low-calorie refresher. Serve it in mugs with paprika-tipped cucumber wedges as stirrers.

Apricot-Buttermilk Pie

Brightly hued apricot filling nestles beneath a delicate buttermilk custard—

  1 cup dried apricot halves
  1½ cups water
  ¼ cup sugar
    Plain Pastry for 1-crust 9-inch
      pie (See *Pastry*)
  2 beaten eggs
  2 cups buttermilk
  ¾ cup sugar

Simmer apricot halves, water, and ¼ cup sugar about 25 minutes. Fit pastry into 9-inch pie plate; crimp edges high.

Blend together beaten eggs, buttermilk, ¾ cup sugar, and dash salt. Spread apricot mixture evenly in bottom of *unbaked* pastry shell. Slowly pour buttermilk filling over apricots. Bake at 400° till knife inserted halfway between the center of the filling and the edge comes out clean, 40 to 45 minutes. Cool.

Cuke-Buttermilk Soup

  2 cucumbers
  ¼ cup snipped parsley
  1 tablespoon chopped green onion
  1 teaspoon salt
    Dash pepper
  1 quart buttermilk

Peel cucumbers; remove and discard seeds. Grate cucumbers. Add parsley, onion, salt, and pepper. Carefully blend in buttermilk. Cover and chill. Makes 4 servings.

BUTTERNUT—A rich, oily nut of a native North American tree of the walnut family, also know as a white walnut. The oblong nut has a hard shell which breaks under a sharp blow often breaking the nutmeats, too. Not marketed commercially, the nuts are available in areas where the trees are grown. This includes New Brunswick west to the Dakotas and Arkansas and south to Georgia. Butternuts are used in cakes and cookies. (See also *Walnut*.)

BUTTERNUT SQUASH—A pear-shaped winter squash with a long neck and a smooth, hard shell. It is one of the turban squashes so named because of the small turbanlike cap at the blossom end. The outside rind ranges in color from dark yellow to tan. The flesh is bright orange and fine grained. Once the seeds have been removed from cut-up squash, pieces are cooked either by baking or steaming and seasoned to taste. Like other winter squash, the butternut variety is an excellent source of vitamin A. (See also *Squash*.)

Butternut Squash Bake

  3 pounds butternut squash
  2 tablespoons butter
  2 teaspoons brown sugar
  ¼ teaspoon salt
  ¼ cup light raisins
  1 tablespoon chopped pecans
  1 tablespoon butter
  1 tablespoon brown sugar
  1 tablespoon light corn syrup
  1 tablespoon chopped pecans

Cut squash in half; do not peel. Remove seeds. Place squash halves cut side down on a baking sheet. Bake at 400° till tender, about 45 minutes. Scoop out pulp. Add next three ingredients; beat well. Stir in raisins and 1 tablespoon chopped pecans.

Turn into 1-quart casserole. Combine butter, brown sugar, and corn syrup; drizzle over squash. Sprinkle with remaining pecans. Bake at 350° for 25 minutes. Makes 4 to 6 servings.

BUTTERSCOTCH—1. A sweet, yet mellow flavor given foods when butter and brown sugar are cooked together. It is a richer and smoother flavor than that obtained by caramelizing sugar. 2. A hard, clear candy also called butterscotch which gets its name from the butter and brown sugar used in its preparation.

A good cook knows her family enjoys butterscotch flavor in cakes, creamy frostings, and as an ice cream topping. Cookies, particularly chewy bar cookies, pack well in lunch boxes or in a picnic basket. Puddings, pie fillings, and many kinds of baked desserts are popular, too. The homemaker may prepare these dishes herself or choose from an ever-increasing variety of packaged mixes, canned puddings, and sauces which are available at the supermarket. There are also handy butterscotch pieces which add butterscotch flavor to cookies and other baked desserts.

Jiffy Butterscotch Torte

    1 package fluffy white frosting
        mix (for 2-layer cake)
    1 teaspoon vanilla
    1 cup graham cracker crumbs
    1 6-ounce package butterscotch
        pieces (1 cup)
    ½ cup flaked coconut
    ½ cup chopped pecans
        Whipped cream

Prepare frosting mix according to package directions; stir in vanilla. Fold in graham cracker crumbs, butterscotch pieces, flaked coconut, and pecans. Turn into greased 9-inch pie plate. Bake at 350° 30 minutes, or till top is lightly browned. Cut in wedges. Serve warm or cool topped with dollops of unsweetened whipped cream. Makes 8 servings.

Sliced or halved Butternut Squash is oven-ready with little effort. Remove seeds. Peel squash before or after cooking, as desired.

Jiffy Butterscotch Torte lives up to its name by making use of fluffy white frosting mix and handy butterscotch pieces.

Butterscotch Sauce

In heavy saucepan, mix 1 slightly beaten egg yolk, ⅔ cup brown sugar, ⅓ cup light corn syrup, ¼ cup butter, and ¼ cup water. Cook and stir over low heat till thick. Stir before using. Makes 1 cup sauce.

Butterscotch Bars

     ½ cup butter or margarine
     2 cups brown sugar
     2 eggs
     1 teaspoon vanilla
     2 cups sifted all-purpose flour
     2 teaspoons baking powder
     ¼ teaspoon salt
     1 cup flaked coconut
     1 cup chopped walnuts

In 2-quart saucepan, melt butter. Remove from heat; stir in brown sugar. Add eggs, one at a time, beating well after each addition; add vanilla. Sift together dry ingredients; add with coconut and nuts to brown sugar mixture. Mix thoroughly. Spread in greased 15½x10½x 1-inch baking pan. Bake at 350° about 25 minutes. Cut in bars while warm. Makes 3 dozen.

Sprinkle crunchy chopped walnuts on individual servings of Butterscotch Puffs before baking this family-pleasing dessert.

Butterscotch Drops

     ½ cup butter or margarine
     ½ cup brown sugar
     2 eggs
     ¼ cup milk
   1¾ cups prepared biscuit mix
     1 cup bran flakes
     ½ cup chopped walnuts
     ½ cup raisins
     ¼ teaspoon ground cinnamon
     ¼ teaspoon ground nutmeg

Cream butter and sugar; beat in eggs and milk. Stir in remaining ingredients. Drop from teaspoon on ungreased cookie sheet. Bake at 375° for 10 minutes. Makes 4 dozen cookies

Butterscotch Puffs

     ¼ cup butter or margarine
     ¾ cup brown sugar
     ¼ teaspoon salt
   1¾ cup milk, scalded
     3 beaten egg yolks
     1 teaspoon vanilla
     3 stiff-beaten egg whites
     ⅓ cup chopped walnuts

Cream together butter or margarine, brown sugar, and salt till mixture is light and fluffy. Blend a small amount of hot milk into beaten egg yolks; gradually stir in remaining milk. Stir in vanilla. Add to creamed mixture, blending thoroughly. Fold into beaten egg whites.

Set eight 5-ounce custard cups in a shallow baking pan. Pour custard mixture into the cups; top with chopped walnuts. Place pan in oven. Pour hot water into pan around custard cups until about 1-inch deep. Bake at 325° till knife inserted just off center comes out clean, about 45 minutes. Serve dessert warm or chilled. Makes 8 servings.

BUTTON MUSHROOMS—A size designation for small fresh or canned mushrooms whose caps measure about one-half inch in diameter. In appearance they resemble rounded buttons, hence the name. Because of their attractive size, button mushrooms are generally used whole in salads, sauces, and casseroles. (See also *Mushroom*.)

C

CABBAGE—A fleshy-leafed member of the mustard family with an astonishingly large botanical family. Besides the familar headed green and red varieties, better-known members are Chinese and Savoy cabbage, kale, collards, kohlrabi, broccoli, cauliflower, and Brussels sprouts.

Exact origin of the cabbage is lost in antiquity, but leafy varieties were known to exist in southern Europe over 4,000 years ago. And it has been known to exist thousands of years in the Orient, too. As history records, early Greeks and Romans enjoyed cabbage both raw and cooked. In fact Cato, the Roman statesman, devoted five pages to cabbage in his book on agriculture. The ancient Egyptians went much further by considering cabbage a god to be worshiped at a special altar. Although the Romans took credit for developing a type of headed cabbage, the actual hard-headed cabbage varieties were unknown until after the ninth century A.D.

Explorers are believed to have carried cabbage and cabbage seeds to northern and central Europe hundreds of years ago. Jacques Cartier is said to have planted cabbage in Canada in the mid-sixteenth century, and it was undoubtedly planted in America by early colonists. Because it adapts well to all kinds of climate and soil, some form of cabbage is served in almost every country in the world today.

Nutritional value: Raw cabbage contains large amounts of vitamin C and ranks with citrus fruits as a major source of this nutrient. The amount of this water-soluble vitamin in cooked cabbage depends upon how much liquid is used and the length of cooking time. A variety of vitamins and minerals in lesser amounts make cabbage a valuable menu addition. One cup of shredded cabbage contains 24 calories.

Types of cabbage: This popular vegetable is available in most markets all year round in different types of heads according to the season. Early or "new" cabbage comes to market in the spring and has a fairly small pointed or conical head with green leaves. Its season is relatively short since this cabbage does not store well. The late-maturing, solid-headed cabbage, used for storage and prolonged marketing, has round or oval heads. It is smooth, solid, and heavy with close, overlapping leaves. The color is light green. Mid-season cabbages have less compact, flat or round heads with somewhat crumply leaves of pale green. Storage time is short, with marketing during the fall or late summer.

Red cabbage, available in compact round or pointed heads, is prized for its distinctive dark red to purple color. It is generally available in supermarkets from late summer to early winter.

Savoy cabbage with its large, rich green, crinkly leaves is easily distinguishable. The heads are loosely formed, usually flattened, and look like big frilly flowers.

There are two types of cabbage referred to as Chinese cabbage. Both have what might be called oval heads with leafy stalks. One, also known as celery or long cabbage, has thick, compact white stalks that are topped with light green, fringed leaves. This variety has gained enough popularity so that produce counters in supermarkets across the country carry it. Chinese names for this vegetable are *pe-tsai*, *wong bok*, and *sin choy*.

The Chinese cabbage called *bok choy* or *bok toy* resembles chard more than celery. Stalks are white, less compactly bunched than celery, and the leaves are deep green, large and somewhat ruffled. It is usually found only in Chinese markets.

Brussels sprouts, little cabbages, are obvious members of the family. However, because broccoli, cauliflower, collard, kale, and kohlrabi differ so in shape, many homemakers are surprised at the broad family relationship.

How to select and store: Any head of cabbage should be well trimmed, reasonably solid, and heavy for its size. Leaves should be good color for the variety and free from signs of insect damage or bruises and tears. Avoid the soft, puffy head or those with yellow or withered leaves. A head that shows one or more deep cracks has been overgrown before picking and will lack the best eating quality.

Cabbage should be stored in the refrigerator in a covered container or covered in foil or plastic wrap. Sprinkling with water helps prevent wilting and drying of outer cabbage leaves during storage.

One pound of cabbage yields about 3½ cups of raw shredded cabbage, or 2 to 2½ cups of the vegetable when cooked.

Colorful cabbage

← Gaily patterned red cabbage wedges and delicate green cabbage heads are as versatile in salads as they are attractive.

How to use: Cabbage is enjoyed both cooked and raw. Sometimes shredded, sometimes cut in wedges, it appears in many kinds of dishes of differing national backgrounds. There are hot and cold salads of German descent, vegetable medleys with an oriental influence, and hearty stuffed cabbage leaves from many lands.

Short-time cooking is best for cabbage. Overcooking makes it unpleasantly strong in flavor and causes loss of color and nutritional value. Strong cabbage odor can be lessened and the good flavor maintained if the cover of the pan in which the cabbage is cooked is removed during the first five minutes of cooking.

To keep the rich color in red cabbage, lemon juice or vinegar is added to the cooking water to make the liquid slightly acid. Red cabbage turns purple blue in neutral water and an unpleasant green-shade in alkaline cooking water.

Pennsylvania Red Cabbage

2 tablespoons bacon drippings
4 cups shredded red cabbage
2 cups cubed unpeeled apple
¼ cup brown sugar
¼ cup vinegar
1¼ teaspoons salt
½ teaspoon caraway seed
Dash pepper

Heat bacon drippings in skillet; add remaining ingredients and ¼ cup water. Cook, covered, over low heat; stir occasionally. For crisp cabbage, cook 15 minutes; for more tender cabbage, 25 to 30 minutes. Makes 4 or 5 servings.

Varying amounts and kinds of liquid are used in cooking cabbage. Panned or steamed cabbage is cooked till crisp-tender using a little butter or margarine and just the water that clings to the freshly washed leaves as moisture. Bacon drippings substituted for the butter contribute their own distinctive smoked flavor to the finished dish. Country-style cabbage has cream added just before serving. Wedges of cabbage are often added to the broth in which corned beef is cooked. Or, they

may be cooked in a small amount of boiling salted water and served with a cheese sauce. Sometimes other vegetables are cooked with the cabbage. Celery, green pepper, and carrots are colorful choices.

Panfried Cabbage

In skillet fry 3 slices bacon till crisp-cooked; remove bacon and crumble. Drain and reserve fat; return 2 tablespoons fat to skillet. Toss 4 cups shredded cabbage in hot fat. Cook over low heat, stirring occasionally until tender, about 10 minutes. Add 1 tablespoon lemon juice, ¼ teaspoon salt, and dash pepper. Garnish with crumbled bacon. Serves 4 to 6.

Country-Style Cabbage

Melt ¼ cup butter or margarine in skillet with ½ teaspoon salt and dash pepper. Add 1 medium head cabbage, shredded (8 cups); cover and cook 5 to 6 minutes stirring occasionally. Blend ¼ cup light cream into mixture. Cook 2 minutes longer or till mixture is heated through. Makes 6 to 8 servings.

Emerald Cabbage

> 2 tablespoons butter or margarine
> 3 cups shredded cabbage (about ½ small head)
> 1 cup sliced celery
> ½ cup sliced green pepper
> ¼ cup sliced onion
> ½ teaspoon salt
> Dash pepper

Melt butter in a skillet; add cabbage, celery, green pepper, onion, salt, and pepper. Cover and cook vegetables over low heat 10 to 12 minutes, stirring mixture occasionally. Serve at once. Makes 6 servings.

Stuffed cabbage leaves

←Swedish Cabbage Rolls are typical of the many national dishes featuring cabbage leaves filled with tasty meat stuffings.

Vegetable Chow Mein

> ¼ cup butter or margarine
> 3 cups coarsely shredded cabbage (about ½ small head)
> 1 cup bias-cut celery slices
> 1 cup thinly sliced carrot rounds
> 1 green pepper, cut in strips
> ½ cup chopped onion
> 1 teaspoon salt
> Dash pepper
> 1 6-ounce can evaporated milk (⅔ cup)

Melt butter in large skillet; add cabbage, celery, carrots, green pepper, onion, salt, and pepper. Cover and cook over medium heat just till vegetables are crisp-tender, about 5 minutes. Add milk; heat thoroughly, stirring gently once or twice. Serves 6.

Swedish Cabbage Rolls

> 1 egg
> ⅔ cup milk
> ¼ cup finely chopped onion
> 1 teaspoon salt
> 1 teaspoon Worcestershire sauce
> Dash pepper
> ½ pound ground beef
> ½ pound ground pork
> ¾ cup cooked rice
> • • •
> 6 large cabbage leaves
> 1 10¾-ounce can condensed tomato soup
> 1 tablespoon brown sugar
> 1 tablespoon lemon juice

In a bowl combine egg, milk, onion, salt, Worcestershire sauce, and pepper; mix well. Add ground beef, ground pork, and cooked rice; beat together with fork. Immerse cabbage leaves in boiling water for 3 minutes or just till limp; drain. Heavy center vein of leaf may be slit about 2½ inches. Place ½ cup meat mixture on each leaf; fold in sides and roll ends over meat. Place stuffed cabbage rolls in 12x 7½x2-inch baking dish.

Blend together soup, brown sugar, and lemon juice; pour over cabbage rolls. Bake at 350° for 1¼ hours. Baste once or twice with tomato sauce. Makes 6 servings.

Use a sharp knife to cut even shreds for coleslaw or panned cabbage. First cut head in quarters, then hold firmly to slice.

When a fine, juicy slaw is desired, place shredded cabbage in salad bowl, then chop finely with a three-edged chopper.

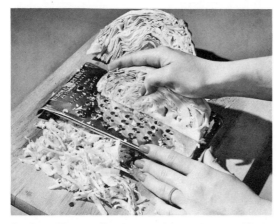

A shredder makes fine, short shreds. Hold it over a bowl or on cutting board and push quarter heads of cabbage across.

Cheese-Sauced Cabbage

Cut 1 medium head cabbage in 6 to 8 wedges. Cook in small amount boiling salted water 10 to 12 minutes; drain well. Pour cheese sauce over cabbage. Makes 6 to 8 servings.

Cheese Sauce: Melt 2 tablespoons butter in saucepan over low heat. Blend in 2 tablespoons all-purpose flour, $\frac{1}{4}$ teaspoon salt, and dash white pepper. Add 1 cup milk all at once. Cook, stirring constantly, till thickened and bubbly. Remove from heat. Stir in 2 ounces shredded process American cheese ($\frac{1}{2}$ cup).

Peppy Cabbage

   5 **cups shredded cabbage**

   . . .

   3 **tablespoons butter, melted**
   1 **teaspoon lemon juice**
   1 **teaspoon prepared horseradish**
$\frac{1}{2}$ **teaspoon salt**
$\frac{1}{2}$ **teaspoon sugar**

Cook cabbage, covered, in 1 quart boiling salted water 7 minutes; drain well. Combine remaining ingredients; toss gently with cooked cabbage. Makes 4 to 6 servings.

Cabbage Bowls

Loosen outer green leaves of large head of cabbage but *do not* break off. Cut remainder of head in 8 sections *halfway* down. Hollow out center, leaving shell of 6 to 8 leaves. Place upside down in ice water to crisp. Drain. Shred center for slaw; refill bowl.

Or, make bowl by loosening outer leaves; spread out petal fashion. Hollow out center to within 1 inch of sides and bottom. Shred center for slaw. Refill bowl with slaw.

Zippy Mustard Slaw

Combine 4 cups shredded cabbage, $\frac{1}{2}$ cup diced cucumber, $\frac{1}{2}$ cup diced celery, and $\frac{1}{4}$ cup chopped green pepper; chill well. Blend thoroughly $\frac{1}{2}$ cup mayonnaise, 2 tablespoons prepared mustard, $\frac{1}{4}$ teaspoon salt, and $\frac{1}{4}$ teaspoon paprika. Pour dressing over chilled vegetables; toss lightly. Makes 6 servings.

Bits of sliced green onion are tossed with the crisp cabbage in this Creamy Cabbage Slaw. A peppy celery seed dressing coats each piece. The salad can be made with red cabbage, too.

Creamy Cabbage Slaw

6 cups shredded cabbage
¼ cup sliced green onion
1 cup mayonnaise or salad
   dressing
2 tablespoons sugar
2 tablespoons vinegar
2 teaspoons celery seed
1 teaspoon salt

Combine shredded cabbage and sliced green onion; chill. Blend together mayonnaise or salad dressing, sugar, vinegar, celery seed, and salt, stirring till sugar is dissolved; chill. Toss the seasoned mayonnaise lightly with cabbage mixture. Makes 10 servings.

Polynesian Coleslaw

Combine 2 cups shredded lettuce, 2 cups shredded cabbage, and ½ cup chopped unpeeled cucumber; chill. Pour 2 tablespoons milk over ¼ cup flaked coconut; let stand 10 minutes. Blend together ⅔ cup mayonnaise, ¼ teaspoon salt, and dash pepper; stir in coconut. Toss dressing with vegetables. Serves 5 or 6.

Cabbage is most often served shredded or chopped in a crisp salad. Some coleslaw lovers choose a vinegar and oil dressing for the salad. Others prefer mayonnaise. (See *Chinese Cabbage, Coleslaw, Salad, Vegetable* for additional information.)

Create a Caesar Salad right at the table. Drizzle oil and vinegar over romaine. Squeeze juice from a lemon with the aid of a fork.

Break coddled eggs (placed one minute in boiling water in covered pan) over salad. Season with salt and Worcestershire sauce.

Grind pepper over salad, sprinkle with Parmesan cheese and crisp croutons. Roll-toss salad with flourish and serve as the entrée.

CABBAGE PALM — Palm trees having terminal leaf buds which resemble cabbages. Sections of the palm are used as vegetables, in salads, or as garnishes. Fresh cabbage palms are available only in tropical areas. However, canned heart of palm (the tender center of cabbage palm) is sold in many markets. (See also *Heart of Palm*.)

CABINET PUDDING — Bread or cake pudding that can be made with stale crumbs or from lady fingers and is filled with candied fruit, raisins, and currants. Bake it in a mold placed in a larger pan which holds an inch of hot water. Serve with a fruit sauce. (See also *Dessert*.)

CACTUS PEAR — Oval fruit of cactus plants. This sweet, juicy fruit is also known as prickly pear. (See also *Prickly Pear*.)

CAESAR SALAD — Salad made with romaine, coddled eggs, garlic, oil, lemon juice, croutons, and cheese. Anchovies, not an original ingredient, are sometimes added.

The familiar emergency situation of hungry people to feed and little food in the kitchen prompted the creation of this famous salad. A restaurateur in Tijuana, Mexico, when faced with this problem, concocted a salad with the ingredients he had on hand. With a flourish he tossed all these together in front of the guests and created the original Caesar salad.

Serve Caesar salad immediately after the ingredients are combined. Either toss it in the kitchen and bring to the table, or roll-toss it right at the table.

Original Caesar Salad

3 medium heads romaine, chilled
About ⅓ cup Garlic Olive Oil
2 to 3 tablespoons wine vinegar
1 lemon, halved
1 or 2 1-minute coddled eggs
Dash Worcestershire sauce
6 tablespoons grated Parmesan
cheese

. . .

About 1 cup Caesar Croutons

Break romaine leaves in 2- or 3-inch widths into chilled salad bowl. Drizzle with Garlic Olive Oil, then vinegar. Squeeze lemon over; break in coddled eggs.

Season with salt and Worcestershire sauce. Grind pepper over all. Sprinkle with grated Parmesan cheese. Roll-toss 6 or 7 times, or till dressing is well combined and every leaf is coated. Add Caesar Croutons; toss once or twice. Serve *at once* on chilled dinner plates. Garnish with rolled anchovies, if desired. Makes 6 servings as the main course.

Garlic Olive Oil: Prepare one to several days early. Slice 6 cloves of garlic lengthwise in quarters; let stand in 1 cup olive oil (or salad oil or half of each).

Caesar Croutons: Cut each slice of bread in 5 strips one way, then across 5 times to make cubes. Spread out on baking sheet; pour a little Garlic Olive Oil over cubes. Heat at 225° for 2 hours. Sprinkle with grated Parmesan cheese. Store in covered jar in the refrigerator.

Café de Belgique, an exotic coffee drink, adds the final touch to a dinner party or a special touch to simple refreshments.

Roll-tossing is accomplished by holding the salad fork and spoon and gently stroking downward to the bottom of the bowl with one tool while going up-and-over with the other tool. (See also *Salad.*)

CAFÉ *(ka fā')*—A French term for coffee. Also, a name for a small restaurant.

Café de Belgique

½ cup whipping cream
¼ teaspoon vanilla
1 stiffly beaten egg white
Strong hot coffee

Combine cream and vanilla; beat till soft peaks form. Fold into beaten egg white. Fill four coffee cups about ¼ full with cream mixture. Pour in coffee. Serve at once. Pass sugar; sweeten to taste. Makes 4 servings.

CAFÉ AU LAIT *(kaf' ā ō lā', ka fā-')*—A drink of hot coffee and scalded milk combined in equal amounts. Usually these two ingredients are poured into the coffee cups at the same time.

Café au Lait

Brew coffee regular strength. Heat equal parts of milk and light cream over low heat. Beat with rotary beater till foamy. Transfer to warmed container. Pour hot coffee and hot milk mixture together into serving cups.

CAFÉ BRÛLOT *(kaf' ā brōō lō')*—After-dinner drink made of strong coffee, liquor, and spices. Brandy, sugar, lemon and orange rind, cloves, and cinnamon are used to flavor the coffee. *Café Brûlot* is traditionally served in tall, narrow cups and flamed briefly just before serving.

CAFFEINE *(ka fēn', kaf' ēn)* — Alkaloid found in coffee, tea, and kola nut. This substance is bitter, a stimulant, and a diuretic. The amounts consumed in coffee, tea, chocolate, and cocoa are usually nontoxic and mildly stimulating.

CAKE

*How to bake perfect cakes every time
using basic ingredients or convenience products.*

This sweet, breadlike dessert is a favorite American food that has become an integral part of many celebrations. What would a birthday party or wedding reception be without the traditional cake?

Cake's role in our society can be traced far back into history. Ancient Egyptians recorded over 30 different cakes and breads in use during the Twentieth Dynasty. Romans, as early as the second century B.C., treasured a fruitcake, "satura," made with barley mash, raisins, pine kernels, pomegranate seeds, and honeyed wine.

The origin of many cakes is unknown, but a few can be traced to individuals, bakeries, or food companies. For instance, sponge cake originated in the Italian House of Savoy during the eleventh century. The recipe was introduced to many countries during the thirteenth century by the daughters of this house when they married and moved to foreign lands.

Angel cake is another cake with a known history. It was first made in 1890 in a St. Louis restaurant. The chef guarded the secret of this high, light cake by insisting that he used a special powder. It was later discovered that cream of tartar was this secret ingredient.

The newest type of cake, chiffon, is made with salad oil and was developed in 1949 by a flour milling company.

Cake baking has always been a fulfilling art. Even when beating ingredients for hours and guessing at oven temperatures

was necessary, women enjoyed making a cake. Modern appliances, improved products, mixes, and tested recipes have taken away much of the labor and the trial and error. However, a homemaker today is still justifiably proud of a beautiful, fragrant, delicious cake made for the family or friend's eating enjoyment.

There's no secret to baking perfect cakes. One must simply follow directions, measure accurately, and time carefully.

Select only recipes from sources that carefully test the recipes or select mixes from reputable companies. When using a recipe, follow the directions exactly. In general, alter amounts or kinds of ingredients or pan sizes only when using standard substitutions. Follow the order and method of mixing, for a change can upset the carefully balanced ingredients.

Many cake mixes have considerable tolerance in their formulas so that flavorings and fruits or nuts can be added. Suggestions often appear on the package.

Basic cake ingredients: Cakes are made from a combination of flour, sugar, eggs, leavening, liquid, fat, and flavoring.

Flour gives the cake structure by building a framework. Both cake flour and all-purpose flour are used in cakes. Cake flour produces a larger, softer, more velvety cake than all-purpose. However, all-purpose is more nutritious. When a recipe does not specify which type to use, assume all-purpose is to be used. If a substitution is necessary, use the formula, one cup of cake flour equals one cup minus two tablespoons of all-purpose flour.

Recipes usually call for a cup measure of sifted flour. To measure this correctly, sift the flour, spoon it lightly into an individual measuring cup, and level off with

Birthday cake and ice cream

←Freeze Pink Lemonade Cake until time to serve. Yellow cake layers made from a cake mix are filled with tinted vanilla ice cream.

a spatula or the flat side of a knife. Never pack the sifted flour or shake the cup; this will result in too much flour in the cup and thus a poor cake.

Cakes are sweetened by granulated, brown, or confectioners' sugar. Generally, granulated sugar is used unless stated otherwise. Measure all of these in individual measuring cups and level off. Brown sugar should be packed into the cups and confectioners' sugar should be sifted.

Another major ingredient, eggs, adds flavor and richness as well as giving volume to cakes. Use medium or large eggs since this is how most recipes are tested. Whites and yolks can be beaten to incorporate air which leavens the cake.

Leavening, the substance which causes a food to rise, makes the cake lighter, more digestible, and more palatable. Baking powder is normally used, but air incorporated in eggs, steam from liquid in the cake, and the reaction of baking soda and acid in a liquid also leavens the cake.

Milk, water, fruit juice, buttermilk, and sour milk are the liquids generally used in a cake. Always measure a liquid in a glass measuring cup placed on a level surface. Bend down to eye level to see if the liquid reaches the correct line.

There are several fats that can be used in a cake—shortening, butter, margarine, and salad oil. Each will give flavor and tenderness. Measure shortening in individual measuring cups and make sure all air bubbles are pressed out.

A second method of measuring shortenings is water displacement. This can be used when the water that clings to the shortening will not affect the product. To measure, pour cold water into a glass cup to the mark which will equal one cup when the desired amount of fat is added. For example, if one-fourth cup of shortening is needed, pour three-fourths cup of water into the cup. Add enough shortening to the water to make the water level rise to the one cup mark, making sure that the shortening is entirely covered with water. Then, drain off the water.

Butter and margarine come in conveniently marked wrappers so that the exact amount can be cut off. Salad oil should be measured in glass cups like other liquids.

How to prepare: Once a cake recipe or mix has been selected, organize the plan, the ingredients, and the tools. Then proceed with the directions adhering to the basic rules of good cake baking.

Study the recipe carefully. Check to see that all ingredients are on hand in the amount needed. Be sure the pans are available in the correct size. Review the directions to see that each step is understood and the organization is clear.

Set out all ingredients unless the recipe specifically states that one should be cold. Generally, ingredients mix and blend better when at room temperature. Eggs are beaten to greater volume when at room temperature, but separate easier when cold. Therefore, separate the yolks from the whites if necessary when you first remove them from the refrigerator rather than at mixing time. Get out all appliances, mixing bowls, measuring utensils, and baking pans. Grease and flour or line pans with waxed paper as the recipe directs. Don't forget to preheat the oven.

Now that all the ingredients and utensils are ready, the cake can be mixed quickly and easily. Pour the batter into the prepared pans as soon as it's mixed. Place pans in the preheated oven as near the center as possible. Stagger pans, if necessary, to get several into the oven. When pans are placed on two racks, do not set one directly above another. Never let pans touch each other or the oven wall. There should be some space around the sides of each pan for even heat and air circulation to assure even browning.

Time the baking carefully and do not open the oven door until the minimum time has elapsed. The cake is done when the sides begin to shrink away from the pan, the cake springs back when lightly touched on the top leaving no imprint, or when a wooden pick inserted in the center of the cake comes out clean and dry.

Raspberries are fresh or frozen

Timesaving Angel-Berry Cake can be made → with either a purchased cake or mix. Serve it cold for a refreshing summer dessert.

Packaged cake mixes have already completed the first steps of measuring and sifting dry ingredients and of blending in the shortening. From this point, simply proceed with the manufacturer's directions for adding ingredients, mixing speeds, and length of mixing and baking time to make a delightful cake. If desired, additional ingredients can be added to this basic cake or it can be baked in various shapes for a more elaborate product.

How to store: Keep the cake moist by covering it with a cake cover or a large, deep bowl, and place a piece of waxed paper or clear plastic wrap over the cut edges for extra protection. A frosting on the cake will help to keep it moist.

Refrigerate cakes which have ingredients that require a cool temperature, such as whipped cream and cream fillings. Fruitcakes are usually covered with cheesecloth, foil, or clear plastic wrap.

Cakes freeze well and can be stored for several months. Seal the unfrosted cakes in moisture-vaporproof freezer wrap when completely cool and place in the freezer.

Cakes frosted with a butter, fudge, confectioners' sugar, or penuche frosting freeze well. Frosting made with egg whites, such as seafoam or seven-minute, do not freeze satisfactorily. Place the cake on a plate or heavy piece of cardboard which is covered with foil or wrapping paper.

Improvise a cake cooler for chiffon or angel cakes baked in tube pans. Turn cake upside down on the neck of a sturdy bottle to cool.

This serves as a holder and does not take up freezer space or tie up serving dishes. Set the cake in the freezer just long enough to harden the frosting, then wrap.

When thawing, loosen the wrapping slightly to form a tent over the cake. This procedure will prevent moisture from collecting on the cake and the frosting from sticking to the wrapping, yet will keep it moist. Cakes thaw in one to four hours.

How to serve: Cakes are used primarily as desserts but are also popular as formal or informal refreshments and snacks.

Serve the cake plain or with a frosting, whipped cream, or fruit. Most cakes are so adaptable that a single cake can be served in a variety of ways. A cake can be eaten in its original form, and if any is left, it can be topped later with a sauce or ice cream for a new dessert. If the cake has become stale it can be used in making puddings or toasted and spread with butter or cream cheese for a sandwich.

Slice a cake with a thin, sharp knife or a cake breaker. Foam cakes can be pulled apart with two forks.

Foam cakes

True foam cakes are leavened by the air incorporated into the eggs, and have no shortening. Sometimes baking powder is added for leavening in addition to the leavening which comes from the eggs. Examples of this category are sponge cake, angel cake, pound cake, jelly roll, ladyfinger, and chiffon cake. Chiffon cake, made with salad oil, is not a true foam cake but rather a cross between a light foam cake and a rich shortened cake.

Foam cake ingredients are usually flour, eggs, sugar, salt, cream of tartar, and flavoring. Cake flour is preferred for its tenderness. Egg whites are often measured in cups rather than by number of whites for a more accurate measure. Cream of tartar stabilizes the egg white foam.

Mixing method: Basic methods of mixing foam cakes begin with beating egg whites till soft peaks form, after adding cream of tartar and salt. Sugar and flavorings are then beaten in. Flour and the remaining

Hollow-out an angel cake and fill with a lemon pudding mixture. Lemon Glow Angel Cake is made from mixes kept on hand.

sugar are sifted together so they will be thoroughly mixed. The flour mixture is sprinkled or sifted over and folded into the whites. To fold, cut down through the mixture with a rubber scraper, go across bottom of bowl, up and over, close to surface; mix thoroughly but gently. Folding is sometimes done on the low speed of an electric mixer to save time and work.

The sequence of adding ingredients in sponge and chiffon cakes varies slightly from this basic method. For a sponge cake, egg yolks are beaten till thick and folded into the stiffly beaten egg whites. Then the flour and sugar mixture is folded in. For a chiffon cake, the salad oil, egg yolks, and flavorings are added to the dry ingredients. These are beaten smooth and folded into stiffly beaten egg whites.

Pour the foam cake batter into an ungreased pan (jelly rolls are an exception, they are baked in greased pans) so that the cake can "climb" the sides of the pan. Carefully move a spatula through the batter to remove any large air bubbles or air tunnels, but do not bang or tap the pan.

After the cake has been baked, turn it upside down to cool until the structure becomes firm. If removed before cool, the cake may collapse. Fit the tube of the pan over an inverted funnel or the neck of a sturdy bottle for cooling if the pan does not have legs for a support.

Characteristics: Perfect foam cakes are light, tender, and moist, but never sticky. Cells in the structure are uniform and medium-sized. The cake pulls apart easily. Flavor and aroma are pleasant, delicate, and typical of ingredients added. If the cake does not meet these standards see *Angel Food Cake* for causes of failure.

Frosting: Foam cakes can be frosted with thin glazes or a soft whipped frosting which matches the cake's light texture.

Almond Coffee Roll

       3 egg whites
    1/4 teaspoon cream of tartar
    3/4 cup sugar
       3 egg yolks
    1/2 teaspoon vanilla
    1 1/2 teaspoons instant coffee powder
       1 cup sifted all-purpose flour
    1 1/2 teaspoons baking powder
    1/4 teaspoon salt
          Sifted confectioners' sugar
          Whipped cream
          Toasted almonds

Place egg whites and cream of tartar in large bowl; beat till soft peaks form. Gradually add 1/4 *cup* sugar, beating till stiff peaks form. Place egg yolks in another bowl; beat till thick. Gradually add remaining sugar to yolks and beat till very thick; beat in vanilla. Dissolve coffee in 1/2 cup water. Sift flour, baking powder, and salt together; add to yolk mixture alternately with coffee, mixing well after each addition. Fold into whites, a fourth at a time, blend well.

Spread batter in greased and floured 15 1/2x10 1/2x1-inch pan. Bake at 375° till done, about 12 minutes. Loosen sides; turn out onto towel sprinkled with sifted confectioners' sugar. Starting at narrow end, roll cake and towel together; let cool on rack. Unroll; fill with whipped cream and almonds. Roll up. Serves 10.

Frosting Coconut Topped Cupcakes takes only a few seconds—just sprinkle on coconut before baking for a crisp topping.

Coconut Topped Cupcakes

2¼ cups sifted cake flour
1 cup sugar
3 teaspoons baking powder
1 teaspoon salt
⅓ cup salad oil
1 cup milk
1½ teaspoons vanilla
2 egg yolks

•   •   •

2 egg whites
½ cup sugar
1 3½-ounce can flaked coconut

Sift flour, sugar, baking powder, and salt into bowl; make a well in center. Add in order: salad oil, ½ *cup* milk, and vanilla; blend. Beat 1 minute at medium speed on electric mixer. Add remaining milk and egg yolks; beat 1 minute. Beat egg whites till soft peaks form; gradually add ½ cup sugar. Beat till *very stiff peaks* form; fold into batter.

Fill paper bake cups in muffin pans half full. Top with coconut. Bake at 400° about 12 to 15 minutes. Makes about 3 dozen cupcakes.

Tropical Chiffon Cake

2¼ cups sifted cake flour
1½ cups sugar
3 teaspoons baking powder
1 teaspoon salt
½ cup salad oil
¾ cup egg yolks (about 8)
1 teaspoon grated orange peel *or*
  2 teaspoons grated lemon peel
¾ cup orange juice
1 cup egg whites (about 8)
½ teaspoon cream of tartar
1⅓ cups flaked coconut
  Frosting *or* whipped cream

Sift flour, sugar, baking powder, and salt together into bowl. Make well in center. Add in order: oil, egg yolks, peel, and juice. Beat till satin smooth. Beat egg whites with cream of tartar to *very stiff peaks*. Pour batter in thin stream evenly over entire surface of egg whites; fold in gently. Fold in coconut. Bake in *ungreased* 10-inch tube pan at 325° about 55 minutes. Invert pan; cool. Frost with a fluffy frosting or whipped cream.

Lemon Glow Angel Cake

1 3- or 3¼-ounce package *regular* vanilla pudding mix
1 10-inch angel cake
1 21-ounce can lemon pie filling
1 2-ounce package dessert topping mix

Cook pudding according to package directions. Cover surface with waxed paper; cool. With a thin, sharp knife, cut a 1-inch slice from top of cake; lift off and set aside. With knife parallel to sides of cake, cut around cake 1 inch from center hole, and 1 inch from outer edge, leaving "walls" of cake 1 inch thick. Remove center with a fork, leaving a 1 inch thick base. (Do not cut through bottom of cake.)

Beat vanilla pudding till smooth; fold *half* into lemon pie filling. Set aside ½ cup lemon mixture; spoon remaining into cake. Replace top of cake. Prepare topping mix according to package directions; fold in remaining vanilla pudding. Frost top and sides of cake; chill. Before serving, spoon the reserved ½ cup lemon mixture in ring atop cake. Serves 12 to 16.

Black Forest Cake

Incomparable four-layer, chocolate and cherry German cake that's worth the effort—

In mixer bowl beat 2 egg whites till soft peaks form. Gradually add ½ cup sugar, beating till stiff peaks form. Sift together 1¾ cups sifted cake flour, 1 cup sugar, ¾ teaspoon baking soda, and 1 teaspoon salt into mixing bowl. Add ⅓ cup salad oil and ½ cup milk to dry ingredients; beat 1 minute at medium speed on electric mixer. Scrape sides of bowl often.

Add ½ cup milk, 2 egg yolks, and two 1-ounce squares unsweetened chocolate, melted and cooled. Beat 1 minute longer, scraping bowl frequently. Gently fold in egg whites. Pour into two greased and lightly floured 9x1½-inch round pans. Bake at 350° for 30 to 35 minutes. Cool 10 minutes; remove from pans. Cool thoroughly. Split each layer in half making 4 thin layers. Set aside.

Cherry Filling: In mixing bowl combine one 20-ounce can pitted tart red cherries, drained; ½ cup port wine; 1 tablespoon kirsch; and 3 drops almond extract. Chill 3 to 4 hours or overnight. Drain thoroughly.

Chocolate Mousse: Combine three 1-ounce squares semisweet chocolate and 3 tablespoons kirsch in top of double boiler; stir over *hot, not boiling* water till chocolate melts and mixture is smooth. Slowly stir chocolate mixture into 1 well-beaten egg. Whip 1 cup whipping cream and 2 tablespoons sugar; fold into chocolate-egg mixture. Chill 2 hours.

Butter Frosting: Sift one 1-pound package confectioners' sugar (about 4¾ cups). In mixing bowl cream 6 tablespoons butter or margarine; gradually add *half* the sugar, blending well. Beat in 2 tablespoons light cream and 1½ teaspoons vanilla. Gradually blend in remaining confectioners' sugar. Blend in enough light cream (about 2 tablespoons) to make spreading consistency. Chill 30 minutes.

To assemble: Spread ½ cup Butter Frosting on the cut side of a cake layer. With remaining frosting, form one ridge ½ inch wide and ¾ inch high around outside edge of same cake layer; make another ridge 2 inches from outside edge. Chill 30 minutes. Fill spaces with Cherry Filling. Spread second cake layer with Chocolate Mousse and place unfrosted side atop first layer. Chill 30 minutes. Whip 2 cups whipping cream with 2 tablespoons sugar and 1 teaspoon vanilla. Spread third cake layer with 1½ *cups* whipped cream and place atop second layer. Top with fourth cake layer. Reserving ¼ cup whipped cream, frost sides with remainder. Sift confectioners' sugar over top. Garnish with dollops of reserved whipped cream, maraschino cherries, and chocolate curls. Chill 2 hours.

Orange Sunshine Cake

  ¾ cup egg yolks (about 8)
  ⅔ cup sugar
  1 teaspoon grated orange peel
  ½ cup orange juice
  1 cup sifted cake flour
  1 cup egg whites (about 8)
  1 teaspoon cream of tartar
  ⅔ cup sugar

Beat egg yolks till thick and lemon-colored; gradually add ⅔ cup sugar, beating till thick. Combine orange peel and orange juice; add to egg mixture alternately with cake flour, mixing after each addition.

In mixing bowl beat egg whites with cream of tartar and ½ teaspoon salt till soft peaks form. Gradually add ⅔ cup sugar, beating till stiff peaks form. Gently fold into egg yolk mixture. Bake in *ungreased* 10-inch tube pan at 325° for about 1 hour and 10 to 15 minutes. Invert pan; cool completely.

Angel-Berry Cake

  1 10-inch angel cake
  1 pint fresh raspberries, crushed and sweetened with ½ cup sugar *or* 1 10-ounce package frozen raspberries, thawed
  2 cups whipping cream
  ¼ cup sugar
  1 teaspoon vanilla
  6 drops red food coloring

With sharp, thin-bladed knife, make slits at 1-inch intervals around top of cake, between center and rim, cutting through cake from top to bottom. With knife, insert berries into slits. Spoon juice evenly over berries. Whip cream with sugar, vanilla, and food coloring. Frost entire cake with whipped cream. Refrigerate 2 to 3 hours. Makes 8 to 10 servings.

Neapolitan Cake

1 package angel cake mix
½ gallon Neapolitan ice cream
1 4-ounce package dessert topping mix

Prepare and bake cake mix according to package directions; cool inverted. Let ice cream soften at room temperature about 10 to 15 minutes. Slice cake into 4 layers. With knife, cut ice cream into layers according to flavor. Spread chocolate ice cream on bottom cake layer, vanilla on second, and strawberry on third. Stack on serving plate; replace top cake layer. Place in freezer. Prepare topping mix. Frost cake with topping. Freeze 2 to 3 hours.

Shortened cakes

Shortened cakes depend on a leavening agent and air incorporated into the shortening for volume. These cakes cover a wide range—from simple one-egg cakes to elaborate tiered wedding cakes. The infinite variety includes pound, butter, chocolate, spice, fruit, and nut cakes. They are baked in layers, squares, loaves, oblongs, or cupcakes. Gingerbread is a type of shortened cake, and cookies are actually a modified form of the shortened cake.

Shortening, sugar, eggs, flour, liquid, salt, flavoring, and baking powder are the basic ingredients. Nuts; candied, dried, or fresh fruits; and chocolate may be added for additional flavor and texture.

Mixing method: Shortened cakes can be mixed in several ways. There are the conventional, one-bowl, muffin, and pastry-blend methods. Good cake recipes should follow one of these methods. Do not substitute another method for the one used in a recipe since the ingredients are balanced for that particular method.

The conventional method begins by creaming the shortening. Add sugar gradually and beat till light and fluffy. This creates the air bubbles which help to leaven the cake. Blend in the eggs. Occasionally, the sugar or the sugar and eggs are added at the very beginning. Sift dry ingredients together so all are evenly distributed. Add dry ingredients alternately with the liquid, mixing after each addition. Begin and end with the dry ingredients to make a better texture. Stir in fruit or nuts.

One-bowl methods have the dry ingredients and sugar sifted into the bowl. Then the shortening, liquid, and flavoring are added and vigorously beaten. Eggs are added and the mixture is beaten again.

The muffin method is similar to the one-bowl method except that the liquid ingredients are combined and then beaten into the dry ingredients. These cakes are best when warm and will not store well.

The pastry-blend method is the blending of flour, baking powder, salt, and shortening. Blend in sugar and half the liquid. Then blend in eggs and remaining liquid.

Immediately after mixing, pour batter into pans. Recipes usually call for pans which are greased. To grease, rub shortening over bottom of pan with paper toweling or brush on with a pastry brush. Sprinkle a few spoons of flour into the pan and shake the pan to coat the surface with flour. Invert the pan and tap to shake out any excess flour. Or when recipe calls for a lined pan, cut waxed or white paper in the same shape as bottom of the pan. Before placing a pan in the oven, tap the pan on the cabinet top or move spatula through the batter to remove any bubbles.

After baking, cool the cake in the pan placed on a cooling rack for five to ten minutes. Then loosen cake by running a blunt knife around edge, and turn cake out onto a cooling rack. Cool completely before slicing or frosting the cake.

Characteristics: Perfect shortened cakes are slightly rounded on top with a soft, golden brown crust. The cake is light and does not crumble excessively when cut. Grain should be uniform and fine with no large tunnels. Texture is tender and moist. Color and flavor should be rich, pleasant, and appropriate for the ingredients added.

Example of a shortened cake

Create a masterpiece with Yellow Cake Deluxe which features lemon filling, fluffy seven-minute frosting, and coconut garnish.

Stagger cake pans on rack so they will not touch another pan or oven walls. Slide rack out rather than reaching into the hot oven.

Frosting: Shortened cakes are frosted with any type frosting, from a thin glaze to a heavy butter frosting. These cakes are often filled with soft custard, fruit, sauces, and whipped cream. (See *Filling, Frosting* for additional information.)

Creamy White Cake

Fill with lemon pudding for a tart variation—

> 1 cup butter or margarine
> 1¾ cups sugar
> 6 egg whites
> 3 cups sifted cake flour
> 4 teaspoons baking powder
> ¾ teaspoon salt
> ¾ cup milk
> ½ cup water
> 1 teaspoon vanilla

In mixing bowl cream butter or margarine. Add sugar gradually, creaming till light and fluffy. Add egg whites, two at a time, beating well after each addition. Sift together flour, baking powder, and salt. Combine milk, water, and vanilla. Add dry ingredients to creamed mixture alternately with liquid, beginning and ending with dry ingredients. Beat smooth after each addition. Bake in 2 greased and lightly floured 9x1½-inch round pans at 350° till cake tests done, about 30 to 35 minutes. Fill and frost cooled layers with desired frosting.

White Cake Supreme

> ¾ cup shortening
> 1½ cups sugar
> 1½ teaspoons vanilla
> 2¼ cups sifted cake flour
> 3 teaspoons baking powder
> 1 cup milk
> 5 stiffly beaten egg whites

Cream shortening and sugar till light. Add vanilla and mix well. Sift together flour, baking powder, and 1 teaspoon salt. Add to creamed mixture alternately with milk, beating after each addition. Fold in egg whites. Bake in 2 greased and floured 9x1½-inch round pans at 375° for 18 to 20 minutes. Cool 10 minutes; remove from pans. Cool completely and frost.

Yellow Cake

> ⅔ cup butter or margarine
> 1¾ cups sugar
> 2 eggs
> 1½ teaspoons vanilla
> 3 cups sifted cake flour
> 2½ teaspoons baking powder
> 1 teaspoon salt
> 1¼ cups milk

In mixing bowl cream butter or margarine. Add sugar gradually, creaming till light. Add eggs and vanilla and beat till fluffy. Sift flour, baking powder, and salt together; add to creamed mixture alternately with milk, beating after each addition. Beat 1 minute. Bake in 2 greased and floured 9x1½-inch round pans at 350° for 30 to 35 minutes. Cool 10 minutes; remove from pans. Cool completely and frost.

Yellow Cake Deluxe

Prepare Yellow Cake; cool completely. Fill with Lemon Filling, frost with seven-minute frosting, and sprinkle with flaked coconut.

Lemon Filling: Combine ¾ cup sugar, 2 tablespoons cornstarch, and dash salt in saucepan. Add ¾ cup water, 2 slightly beaten egg yolks, and 3 tablespoons lemon juice; cook over medium heat till thick, stirring constantly. Remove from heat; add 1 teaspoon grated lemon peel and 1 tablespoon butter or margarine. Cool.

Best Two-Egg Cake

½ cup shortening
1½ cups sugar
1 teaspoon vanilla
2 eggs
2¼ cups sifted cake flour
2½ teaspoons baking powder
1 cup plus 2 tablespoons milk

Cream shortening and sugar till light, 12 to 15 minutes at medium-high speed on electric mixer. Add vanilla and eggs, one at a time, beating well after each. Sift flour, baking powder, and 1 teaspoon salt together; add to creamed mixture alternately with milk, beating after each addition. Bake in 2 greased and floured 9x1½-inch round pans at 375° for 20 to 25 minutes. Cool 10 minutes; remove from pans. Cool completely and frost, if desired.

Citrus Yellow Cake

⅔ cup shortening
1 tablespoon grated orange peel
1½ teaspoons grated lemon peel
1½ cups sugar
3 eggs
2½ cups sifted cake flour
2½ teaspoons baking powder
2 tablespoons lemon juice
¾ cup milk

Cool shortened cake 10 minutes, loosen edges, place rack over cake, turn all over, and remove pan. To get cake top side up, put second rack on bottom of cake; turn again.

Combine shortening, orange peel, and lemon peel; mix well. Gradually add sugar; cream till light and fluffy. Add eggs, one at a time, beating well after each. Sift together flour, baking powder, and ¾ teaspoon salt; add to creamed mixture alternately with lemon juice and milk, beating smooth after each addition. Bake in 2 greased and floured 9x1½-inch pans at 375° for 25 to 30 minutes. Cool 10 minutes; remove from pans. Cool completely.

Why shortened cakes fail

Shortened cakes, rich, moist, and velvety, are the products of accurately measured ingredients, proper preparation techniques, and carefully followed recipe directions. If a problem should appear in the finished product, one of the following may be the reason:

Coarse texture
Insufficient creaming; oven too slow; not enough liquid.

Heavy, compact texture
Oven too slow; extreme overbeating; too much sugar or shortening.

Dry cake
Overbeaten egg whites; overbaking; too much flour or leavening.

Thick, heavy crust
Baking too long; oven too hot; not enough sugar or shortening.

Hump or cracks on top
Oven too hot; too much flour; pan placed too high in oven.

Moist, sticky crust
Insufficient baking; too much sugar.

Cake falling
Oven too slow; insufficient baking; too much batter in pan; moving cake during baking; too much shortening.

Poor volume
Pan too large; oven too hot; not enough mixing; not enough leavening.

Gingerbread Layer Cake

Abraham Lincoln's favorite Christmas dessert—

  1 cup honey
  1 teaspoon ground ginger
  1 teaspoon ground cinnamon
  ½ teaspoon ground cloves

      . . .

  ½ cup butter or margarine
  ½ cup brown sugar
  ½ teaspoon grated lemon peel
  1 egg
2¼ cups sifted all-purpose flour
  1 teaspoon baking powder
  1 teaspoon baking soda
  ½ teaspoon salt
1¼ cups buttermilk

      . . .

1½ cups whipping cream
  1 tablespoon granulated sugar
  2 teaspoons shredded orange peel
  1 1-ounce square semisweet
     chocolate, grated

In small saucepan combine honey, ginger, cinnamon, and cloves; bring to boiling. Remove from heat; cool. In large mixing bowl cream butter or margarine and brown sugar till light and fluffy. Gradually beat in honey mixture at high speed on electric mixer. Add lemon peel and egg; mix thoroughly.

Sift together flour, baking powder, soda, and salt. Add flour mixture and buttermilk alternately to butter mixture, stirring well after each addition. Pour into 2 greased and lightly floured 8x1½-inch round pans. Bake at 350° for 30 to 35 minutes. Cool in pans 10 minutes. Turn out onto rack and cool.

Just before serving, whip cream with granulated sugar till soft peaks form. Spread one layer with *half* of the whipped cream. Sprinkle with *half* the orange peel and *half* the chocolate. Top with second cake layer. Spread with remaining cream; sprinkle with remaining orange peel and grated chocolate.

Butternut Chocolate Cake

In the Shaker tradition: excellent yet simple—

  1 cup shortening
  2 cups sugar
  2 teaspoons vanilla
  4 1-ounce squares unsweetened
     chocolate, melted and cooled
  5 eggs

      . . .

2¼ cups sifted cake flour
  1 teaspoon baking soda
  1 teaspoon salt
  1 cup sour milk *or* buttermilk
    Chocolate Butter Frosting

Place shortening in bowl. Gradually add sugar, creaming till light and fluffy. Blend in vanilla and cooled chocolate. Add eggs, one at a time, beating well after each. Sift flour, soda, and salt together; add to creamed mixture alternately with sour milk *or* buttermilk, beating after each addition. Pour into 2 well-greased 9x1½-inch round pans. Bake at 350° for 30 to 35 minutes. Cool 10 minutes. Remove from pan and cool completely on cake rack.

Split each layer in half and frost with Chocolate Butter Frosting by spreading ½ cup on each layer and topping with remainder.

Chocolate Butter Frosting: Cream 6 tablespoons butter or margarine; gradually blend in 2 cups sifted confectioners' sugar, beating well. Add 1 egg yolk; one 1-ounce square unsweetened chocolate, melted and cooled; and 1½ teaspoons vanilla. Gradually blend in another 2 cups sifted confectioners' sugar. Add enough milk *or* cream (about ¼ cup) to make frosting of spreading consistency. Trim cake with butternuts or other nutmeats, if desired.

Split cake layers with a sharp, thin-bladed knife. Mark center of layer with wooden picks as a guide for cutting equal halves.

Pink Lemonade Cake

Trim with candy mints or birthday candles—

> 1 package 2-layer-size yellow
>   cake mix
> 1 quart vanilla ice cream
> 1 6-ounce can frozen pink lemonade
>   concentrate, thawed
> 6 drops red food coloring
>
> . . .
>
> 1 cup whipping cream
> 2 tablespoons sugar

Prepare cake mix according to package directions. Bake in two 9x1½-inch round pans; remove from pans and cool. Meanwhile, stir ice cream to soften and quickly stir in ½ *cup* of the lemonade concentrate and food coloring. Spread evenly in foil-lined 9x1½-inch round pan. Freeze 2 or 3 hours or till firm.

Place cake layer on serving plate; top with ice cream layer, then with second cake layer. Whip cream with remaining concentrate and 2 tablespoons sugar till stiff. Frost sides and top of cake; return to freezer at least 1 hour.

Upside-Down Apple Cake

> 3 medium tart apples, peeled,
>   cored, and sliced very thin
> 1 cup apple juice
> ⅓ cup butter or margarine
> 1 cup brown sugar
>
> . . .
>
> 1 package 2-layer-size spice
>   cake mix
>   Maraschino cherry halves
> ½ cup chopped walnuts

Simmer apple slices in apple juice till tender, about 5 minutes. Drain, reserving juice. In 13x9x2-inch pan combine ¼ *cup* reserved hot apple juice, butter, and brown sugar. Place pan in oven till butter melts.

Prepare spice cake mix according to package directions, using remaining reserved apple juice as part of liquid. Arrange apple slices and several maraschino cherry halves in brown sugar mixture; sprinkle with nuts. Spoon batter into pan. Bake at 350° till done, about 45 minutes. Cool 1 to 2 minutes; invert on serving plate. Serve while warm.

Gingerscotch Cake

> 1 package 2-layer-size butterscotch
>   cake mix
> ½ cup chopped walnuts
> 2 tablespoons chopped candied
>   ginger
> 1 1-ounce square semisweet
>   chocolate, grated
>   Whipped cream

Prepare cake mix according to package directions. Stir in chopped walnuts, candied ginger, and grated chocolate. Bake in 2 greased and lightly floured 8x1½-inch round pans at 350° about 35 minutes. Cool 10 minutes; remove from pan. Serve with whipped cream.

Note: Or, bake batter in a greased and lightly floured 13x9x2-inch baking pan for 40 minutes, or till cake tests done.

Berry Meringue Cake

Meringue bakes on top of each layer—

> 1 package 2-layer-size yellow
>   cake mix
> 1⅓ cups orange juice
> 4 egg yolks
> 1½ teaspoons grated orange peel
>
> . . .
>
> 4 egg whites
> ¼ teaspoon cream of tartar
> 1 cup sugar
> 1 pint fresh strawberries
> 2 tablespoons sugar
> 1 cup whipping cream

Combine cake mix, orange juice, egg yolks, and peel; beat 4 minutes at medium speed on electric mixer. Pour into 2 greased and floured 9x1½-inch round pans. Beat egg whites with cream of tartar till soft peaks form; gradually add 1 cup sugar, beating till stiff peaks form. Spread evenly over batter. Bake at 350° for 35 minutes. Cool 10 minutes; remove from pans, meringue side up. Cool completely.

Mash ½ *cup* strawberries with 2 tablespoons sugar; add whipping cream and whip till stiff. Spread ⅔ of cream mixture over bottom layer. Reserving a few whole berries, slice remainder; place over cream mixture. Add top layer; top with remaining cream and reserved berries.

Slice Mother's Best Fudge Cake with knife or cake breaker. Use a sharp, thin-bladed knife for frosted layer cakes. Insert point of knife; keeping point down and handle up, slice with up-and-down motion, pulling knife toward edge of cake. Dip blade in warm water or wipe with damp cloth occasionally to keep free of frosting and crumbs. When using cake breaker, go straight down, then lift up and out of the cake to cut slice. Remove slice with cake server or knife.

Mother's Best Fudge Cake

    1 slightly beaten egg
  ⅔ cup sugar
  ½ cup milk
    3 1-ounce squares unsweetened
        chocolate
    1 cup sugar
  ½ cup shortening
    1 teaspoon vanilla
    2 eggs
    2 cups sifted cake flour
    1 teaspoon baking soda
    1 cup milk
      Chocolate Frosting

In saucepan combine 1 beaten egg, ⅔ cup sugar, ½ cup milk, and chocolate. Cook and stir over medium heat till chocolate melts and mixture comes just to boiling. Cool. Gradually add 1 cup sugar to shortening, creaming till light and fluffy. Add vanilla. Add 2 eggs, one at a time, beating well after each.

Sift together flour, soda, and ½ teaspoon salt; add to creamed mixture alternately with 1 cup milk, beating after each addition. Blend in cooled chocolate mixture.

Bake in 2 greased and floured 9x1½-inch round pans at 350° for 25 to 30 minutes. Cool; frost and fill with Chocolate Frosting. Decorate with chocolate curls, if desired.

Mocha Cupcakes

  ½ cup shortening
    1 cup sugar
    1 egg
    1 teaspoon vanilla
  1⅓ cups sifted all-purpose flour
  ½ cup unsweetened cocoa powder
    1 teaspoon baking powder
  ½ teaspoon baking soda
  ½ cup milk
  1½ teaspoons instant coffee powder

Cream shortening and sugar well. Add egg and vanilla; beat well. Sift flour, cocoa, baking powder, soda, and ¼ teaspoon salt together; beat into creamed mixture alternately with milk. Dissolve coffee in ½ cup hot water; stir into batter. Fill paper bake cups in muffin pan ⅔ full. Bake at 375° for 20 minutes. Cool and frost, if desired. Makes about 18.

Chocolate Fudge Cake

Makes its own frosting while baking—

  1/3 cup shortening
  1 cup sugar
  1/2 teaspoon vanilla
  2 1-ounce squares unsweetened
      chocolate, melted and cooled
  1 egg

  . . .

  1 1/4 cups sifted all-purpose flour
  1/2 teaspoon baking soda
  1/2 teaspoon salt
  3/4 cup water
  1/2 cup semisweet chocolate pieces
  9 walnut halves

Cream shortening and sugar till light and fluffy. Blend in vanilla and cooled chocolate. Add egg, beating well. Sift together flour, soda, and salt; add to creamed mixture alternately with water, beating after each addition. Spread batter in greased and lightly floured 9x9x2-inch baking pan. Sprinkle with chocolate pieces. Arrange walnut halves over top. Bake at 350° till done, about 30 minutes. Cool in pan.

Choco-Cherry Cake

  1/2 cup shortening
  1 cup sugar
  1 egg
  2 1-ounce squares unsweetened
      chocolate, melted

  . . .

  1 1/2 cups sifted cake flour
  1 teaspoon baking soda
  3/4 teaspoon salt
  1 cup milk
  1/4 cup chopped maraschino
      cherries
  2 tablespoons maraschino cherry
      syrup
  1/2 cup chopped walnuts
      No-Cook Fudge Frosting

Place shortening in bowl. Gradually add sugar, creaming till light and fluffy. Add egg; beat well. Stir in melted chocolate.

Sift together flour, baking soda, and salt. Add to creamed mixture alternately with milk, beginning and ending with flour mixture; beat

after each addition. Add cherries, syrup, and chopped nuts. Grease bottom of 8x8x2-inch baking pan; pour in batter. Bake at 350° till cake tests done, about 40 minutes. Cool. Frost in pan with No-Cook Fudge Frosting. Top with walnut halves, if desired.

No-Cook Fudge Frosting: Combine 1 cup sifted confectioners' sugar, 3 tablespoons milk, 1 egg, and 1 teaspoon vanilla in small saucepan (use saucepan for it gives a handle to hold while beating and metal speeds cooling). Mix thoroughly. Stir in two 1-ounce squares unsweetened chocolate, melted and cooled. Add 3 tablespoons *softened* (not melted) butter or margarine, one at a time, beating well after each addition. Chill frosting 10 minutes in refrigerator. Place saucepan in bowl of ice water. Beat frosting till spreading consistency.

Calico Crumb Cake

Tastes like a hot fudge sundae with nut topping—

  1/2 cup sifted all-purpose flour
  1/2 cup brown sugar
  1/4 cup butter or margarine
  1/2 cup finely chopped nuts

  . . .

  2 cups sifted all-purpose flour
  1 cup granulated sugar
  1 teaspoon baking soda
  1 teaspoon salt

  . . .

  1/2 cup shortening
  2 eggs
  1 cup buttermilk *or* sour milk
  2 teaspoons vanilla
  1 6-ounce package semisweet choco-
      late pieces, melted and cooled

Combine 1/2 cup flour and brown sugar; cut in butter or margarine till crumbly. Stir in chopped nuts; set aside. Sift 2 cups flour, granulated sugar, baking soda, and salt into large mixing bowl. Add shortening, eggs, buttermilk *or* sour milk, and vanilla. Blend, then beat at medium speed on electric mixer 2 minutes.

Combine 1 cup batter and the melted, cooled chocolate. Alternate light and dark batters by spoonfuls in greased and lightly floured 13x9x2-inch baking pan; cut through to marble. Sprinkle with reserved crumbly nut mixture. Bake at 350° till done, about 30 minutes. Cool.

Dublin Fruitcake

For Christmas or St. Patrick's Day—

    2 cups butter or margarine
    2 cups sugar
    8 well–beaten eggs
    ½ cup brandy
    1 tablespoon rose water
    1 teaspoon orange extract
        • • •
    4 cups sifted all-purpose flour
    2 teaspoons ground allspice
    1 teaspoon salt
    ½ cup coarsely ground blanched
        almonds
    ¾ cup whole blanched almonds
    3 cups (one 15-ounce package)
        raisins
    3 cups (about 16 ounces) currants
    ¾ cup candied cherries, quartered
    ½ cup chopped candied lemon peel
    ½ cup chopped candied orange peel
        Almond Paste Frosting
        Royal Icing

Cream together butter and sugar. Add eggs, brandy, rose water, and orange extract to creamed mixture, beating till fluffy. Sift together flour, allspice, and salt; stir in ground almonds. Stir flour mixture gently into creamed mixture. Stir in whole almonds, fruits, and peels. Line bottom of a 10-inch springform pan (tube type) with 2 thicknesses of waxed paper; place on baking sheet. Pour batter into pan. Bake at 300° for 2½ hours. Cool in pan on rack. Remove sides of pan; remove cake from pan. Cool completely on rack. Store cake in tightly covered container in cool, dry place. Before serving, frost with Almond Paste Frosting and then with Royal Icing.

Almond Paste Frosting: Place half of an 8-ounce can of almond paste between layers of waxed paper; roll to a 2½-inch wide rectangle, about ⅛ inch thick. Press against side of half the cake; repeat with second half of can of almond paste. Roll another 8-ounce can almond paste to a 10-inch circle, ⅛ inch thick. Cut out a 1½-inch circle from the center. Place 10-inch circle on top of cake. Pat sides and top portions of almond paste together.

Royal Icing: In small mixing bowl combine 3 egg whites (room temperature), one 1-pound package sifted confectioners' sugar (about 4¾

cups), ½ teaspoon cream of tartar, and 1 teaspoon vanilla. Beat with electric mixer 7 to 10 minutes, till very stiff. Keep bowl of frosting covered with damp cloth at all times to prevent crust forming. Makes 3 cups.

Harvest Apple Cake

Flavored with apples, raisins, and walnuts— perfect for early fall—

    2 cups sifted all-purpose flour
    1 cup granulated sugar
    1½ teaspoons baking soda
    1 teaspoon salt
    1 teaspoon ground cinnamon
    ¼ teaspoon ground nutmeg
        • • •
    ¼ cup brown sugar
    ½ cup shortening
    1 cup apple juice
    1½ cups finely chopped peeled
        apples
    2 eggs
    ½ cup raisins
    ½ cup chopped walnuts
        • • •
    2 tablespoons butter or margarine
    1 cup sifted confectioners' sugar
    ½ teaspoon vanilla
    1 to 2 tablespoons apple juice

Sift together flour, granulated sugar, soda, salt, cinnamon, and nutmeg. Stir in brown sugar. Add shortening, 1 cup apple juice, and chopped apple; beat till smooth, about 2 minutes at medium speed on electric mixer. Add eggs; beat well. Stir in raisins and nuts. Bake in greased 13x9x2-inch pan at 350° till cake tests done, about 30 to 35 minutes. Cool.

Meanwhile, make Apple Frosting: beat together butter or margarine, confectioners' sugar, and vanilla. Add 1 to 2 tablespoons apple juice, beating till frosting is of spreading consistency. Frost cooled cake.

It's a great cake for the Irish

Dublin Fruitcake, garnished with sham- →
rocks cut from gumdrops, is served with a beverage of coffee and whipped cream.

Crunchy Apricot Cake

    1 22-ounce can apricot pie filling
    1 package 1-layer-size white
        cake mix
    1 egg
    ½ cup flaked coconut
    ½ cup chopped pecans
    ½ cup butter or margarine, melted

Spread pie filling in bottom of 9x9x2-inch baking dish. In mixing bowl combine cake mix, ⅓ cup water, and egg. Beat 4 minutes at medium speed on electric mixer. Pour over pie filling; sprinkle with coconut and pecans. Drizzle melted butter or margarine over top. Bake at 350° for 40 minutes. Serve warm.

Vanilla Wafer-Coconut Cake

    ½ cup butter or margarine
    1 cup sugar
    1½ cups vanilla wafer crumbs
    ½ teaspoon baking powder
    3 eggs
    1 cup chopped pecans
    1 3½-ounce can flaked coconut
        (1⅓ cups)

In mixing bowl cream butter and sugar till fluffy. Blend in wafer crumbs and baking powder. Beat in eggs, one at a time. Stir in pecans and coconut. Turn into greased and floured 9x1½-inch round baking pan. Bake at 325° for 40 minutes; cool. Cut in 6 to 8 wedges.

Chocolate Date Cake

    1¼ cups boiling water
    ½ pound snipped dates (1½ cups)
    1 package 2-layer-size chocolate
        cake mix
    1 6-ounce package semisweet
        chocolate pieces (1 cup)
    ½ cup chopped walnuts

Pour water over dates; cool. Prepare cake mix following package directions, substituting date mixture for liquid. Turn into greased and floured 13x9x2-inch pan. Top with chocolate pieces and chopped walnuts. Bake at 350° for 35 to 40 minutes. Serve with ice cream.

Pumpkin Spice Cake

    ½ cup shortening
    1⅓ cups sugar
    2 eggs
    1 cup canned pumpkin
    ⅔ cup buttermilk *or* sour milk
    1¾ cups sifted all-purpose flour
    2 teaspoons baking powder
    1 teaspoon baking soda
    1 teaspoon salt
    2 teaspoons ground cinnamon
    ½ teaspoon ground nutmeg
    ¼ teaspoon ground allspice
    ¼ teaspoon ground ginger
        Golden Butter Frosting

Cream shortening and sugar till fluffy. Add eggs, one at a time, beating well after each. Combine pumpkin and buttermilk *or* sour milk. Sift together flour, baking powder, baking soda, salt, cinnamon, nutmeg, allspice, and ginger. Add to creamed mixture alternately with pumpkin mixture, beating well after each addition. Bake in greased and floured 13x9x2-inch pan at 350° for 40 to 45 minutes. Cool; frost with Golden Butter Frosting.

Golden Butter Frosting: Place in small mixing bowl, in order, ½ cup butter or margarine, softened; 1 egg yolk; 2 tablespoons buttermilk *or* milk; ½ teaspoon vanilla; and 3 cups sifted confectioners' sugar. Blend. Beat at medium speed on electric mixer for 3 minutes. Beat in additional sifted confectioners' sugar to make of spreading consistency, if frosting is too soft. Spread on cake.

CAKE BREAKER—A utensil with long prongs which is used for cutting cakes. They are made in stainless steel and sterling silver. Because they do not mash the cake but give a high, fluffy wedge, cake breakers are especially good for cutting foam cakes. To cut a foam cake, press the prongs gently through the cake—turning the handle away from the slice till the cake separates. (See also *Utensil.*)

CAKE COVER—A tall, round cover that fits over a cake. The cover is designed to protect the cake and keep it moist and fresh. Metal, plastic, and glass covers are made in a variety of sizes—10-inch or 14-inch diameter, for example. This cover may fit over a cake plate or fasten onto a base which holds a cake plate. The latter type usually has a carrying handle attached so it can be carried easily to picnics, bake sales, and potluck suppers.

When buying a cake cover, select one which will be large enough to hold eight- and nine-inch cakes plus fluffy frosting. If a commercial cake cover is not available, the cake can be protected and kept fresh for a short time by inverting a deep bowl over the cake and cake plate.

CAKE DECORATING—Adding frosting or trimming in fancy designs to a cake to make it more attractive. Cake decorating ranges from the elaborate, such as a wedding cake with flowers and scrolls of frosting, to the simple, such as cupcakes sprinkled with small decorative candies.

Decorating a cake makes it more appealing. One that is beautifully done arouses more interest, whets the appetite, and adds a special touch to many occasions. Birth-day, wedding, and anniversary cakes, for instance, contribute to the decorations and festive atmosphere of the occasion.

It is easy to see that cake decorating is an art. Those who enjoy creating and displaying a masterpiece realize a special reward for the many hours of work that they've spent in preparing a delicious, attractive cake. Classes, special instructions, and books on cake decorating will help a person learn and perfect this art. As with other arts, practice is necessary to learn and to keep these skills.

Basic materials: Cake decorating is done with a frosted cake, decorating frosting, food coloring, a cone, decorating tubes, flower nail, and, possibly, commercial trims and figures. The frosted cake can be a white, yellow, or chocolate layer cake; an angel food cake; or a chiffon cake. The cake and frosting are primarily intended for eating, so select recipes which make a delicious cake as well as a good foundation for the decorations.

Decorating a cake gives it a personal touch with a professional look. Roses, daisies, and leaves, such as these, can be made by following directions and practicing patiently.

Decorating frosting must be soft enough to go through the tube but firm enough to hold its shape when made into designs. The recipes given here for Ornamental Frosting and Royal Frosting can be used for decorating on the cake or making decorations which will be transferred to the cake. Decorating frosting is also available in plastic tubes and pressurized cans which are sold in supermarkets. These products are usually sold with several decorating tubes and are satisfactory for doing a small amount of decorating.

Frosting may be tinted with liquid, paste, or powdered food coloring. Liquid food coloring can thin the consistency, so allow for this when adding liquid.

A cone to hold the frosting can be constructed from waxed or silicone paper. Canvas and rubber bags are often used for this purpose. Cylinders with plungers are used for cake decorating. However, their use is more limited than bags or cones.

The hole in the decorating tube determines the shape of the frosting. There are numerous types of tubes, but the basic

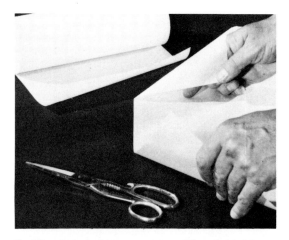

1. For frosting cone, cut a 17x9-inch sheet of silicone paper. Grasp top corners with right hand inside cone, left hand outside.

2. Turn right hand corner over till partial cone is made. Circle right hand with left. Move hands back and forth to make point.

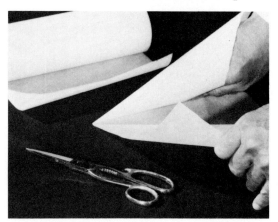

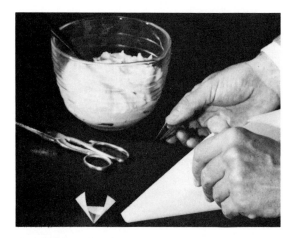

3. Hold top of cone, snip 1¼ to 2 inches from end. Cut straight, not at angle. Drop tube into cone—¾ of tube should protrude.

4. Fill cone ¾ full with decorating frosting. To seal, flatten cone above frosting, fold corners in, fold top down twice.

ones are plain tubes which make simple lines for writing, double line tubes, star tubes, leaf tubes, and flower tubes.

A flower nail resembles a carpenter's nail with a large head—usually one and one-half inches in diameter. This nail can be held and turned in one hand while the frosting cone, held in the other hand, is used to make the flower. The flower is dried before being placed on the cake.

Commercial trims and figures are available in variety stores, supermarkets, and specialty shops for additional decoration.

Ornamental Frosting

A creamy frosting for decorations made directly on the cake—leaves, borders, writing, flowers—

>   1 cup shortening
>   1 teaspoon vanilla
>   4 cups sifted confectioners'
>   sugar
> 1½ tablespoons milk

Blend shortening and vanilla with electric mixer. Slowly add sugar; beat just till combined. Stir in milk. Check frosting consistency by making trial decoration. Add a few drops milk if frosting is too stiff.

Tint to desired color with food coloring. Make decorations on cake or make flowers on silicone or waxed paper. Place flowers on cookie sheet; harden in refrigerator or freezer 1 hour. Transfer to cake with spatula. Work fast to keep flowers cold. Makes 2¼ cups.

Royal Frosting

Very stiff frosting for make-ahead decorations—

Combine 3 egg whites (at room temperature); one 16-ounce package confectioners' sugar, sifted; 1 teaspoon vanilla; and ½ teaspoon cream of tartar. Beat with electric mixer 7 to 10 minutes or till frosting is very stiff. Keep frosting covered with damp cloth at all times to prevent crust from forming. Makes 3 cups.

Make flowers with pastry tube on silicone paper or waxed paper. Let dry 8 hours before peeling off paper. Dab a little frosting on bottom of flower to attach to cake.

Basic procedure: Cake decorating begins with a plan. Select a theme; then plan so that the flavor and color of the cake and frosting, as well as the decorations, will be appropriate to the theme. Avoid a cluttered effect. Having too much on the cake or too many different designs will only spoil the overall effect.

Set up a work schedule so the cake will be ready well ahead of the occasion. The cake can even be baked and frosted a few days ahead and then decorated the day before it is needed. By completing the cake early, you avoid the rush, and still have time to relax and make the other preparations for the party.

First bake and frost the cake. (Follow the general rules for measuring, mixing, and baking.) Remember to cool the cake completely before frosting. While the cake is cooling, prepare a favorite frosting which will form a good background for the decorations. For example, a butter or boiled frosting is a good choice.

To prepare the cooled cake for frosting, set it on the cake plate and arrange strips of waxed paper around the edges so the frosting will not get on the plate. Conceal the hole of a cake baked in a tube pan, if desired, by placing a cardboard circle covered with foil or clear plastic wrap over the center. Frost the cake with a thin layer to hold the crumbs; then cover with a thicker layer. Smooth or swirl the surface of the frosting with a broad spatula or knife to get the effect desired for a background.

Prepare the decorating frosting and assemble the equipment. Make a frosting cone or use a bag or cylinder. Attach the decorating tube and fill the cone with frosting. Practice the design before beginning the actual decorating on the cake. An inverted cake pan the same shape as the cake is a good surface for practicing.

When piping on the frosting, hold the cone at the top with the right hand. This hand applies the pressure. Guide the cone with the first finger of the left hand. One of the most important elements in decorating is maintaining careful control of the squeezing and knowing when to relax pressure on the cone. Now, proceed with the final step of the plan and carefully pipe the design on the cake.

1. *Zigzag border:* Use a No. 30 star tube, or for a broader band, No. 48. Hold cone at a 45° angle to surface. Rest tube lightly on surface and start an even, steady pressure on the cone. Guide the cone in short, side-to-side movements while moving along the line where the border will be.

2. *Shell border:* Use No. 30 star tube. With cone at a 60° angle to cake, rest tube very gently on surface and begin squeezing. As the shell builds up, lift tube about ¼ inch; ease off on the pressure and pull down. The shell comes down to a point by stopping all pressure at the end of the shell.

3. *Reverse shell border:* Similar to shell border except as the shell builds up, guide the cone to the *right* and ease off on the pressure. Guide second shell to the *left*.

4. *Puff border:* Use No. 12 plain tube. Hold cone upright, tube resting lightly on surface. Apply pressure; stop, lifting tube up ¼ inch as frosting builds up. Repeat.

5. *Button border:* Use No. 32 star tube. Hold cone upright, tube resting lightly on cake. Apply pressure; make a *slight* swirling motion. Lift tube ¼ inch from cake. Stop pressure; continue swirl till frosting breaks off.

6. *String-work border:* Use No. 3 plain tube and Ornamental Frosting or slightly thinned Royal Frosting. If frosting is too soft, it will not hold together; if the consistency is too stiff, it will not flow smoothly.

To decorate the cake, touch edge of cake with tube and start squeezing the cone with an even pressure—let gravity pull the string of frosting down. Then move the frosting tube over about 1½ inches. While you squeeze, let the frosting string drop down about 1 inch, and then touch cake edge again. *Keep hand and tube at the top of cake all the time, not following the string.*

Make second row under the first. Bow is a horizontal figure "8" with two short strings attached to complete bow effect.

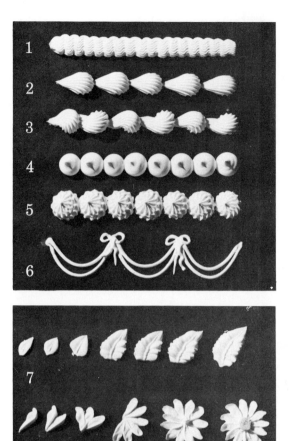

7. *Leaf:* Use No. 67 leaf tube. Fill frosting cone with Ornamental Frosting.

For plain leaves: With cone at a 45° angle, touch cake with tube and apply light pressure; at halfway point of leaf, stop pressure but move tube along, lifting it up slightly till frosting breaks off.

For ruffly leaves: Squeeze and move tube back and forth; diminish pressure near leaf tip; stop pressure; move out to make point.

8. *Daisy:* Put dot of frosting on flower nail and stick a 1½-inch square of waxed paper on top. Then put another frosting dot in center as a target. With wide end of No. 103 rose tube touching paper, start at center of nail and squeeze cone, moving to outer edge; ease off pressure. Turn nail; continue making petals. Pull paper with daisy off nail. When all daisies are made, dot the centers with contrasting color of frosting.

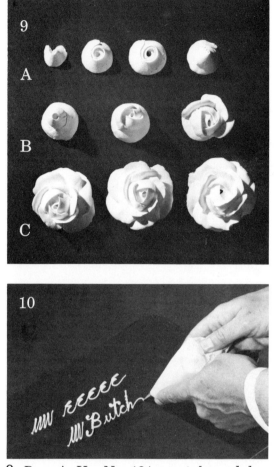

10. *Writing:* Use a No. 3 or 4 plain tube. Fill frosting cone with Ornamental Frosting. Rest tube on surface very lightly. *Relax* and practice with long back-and-forth strokes, using a steady pressure. Then try curved letters, guiding the tube with the left forefinger. When writing on the sides of a cake, place the cake at eye level. It is a good idea to practice writing all the words to be used on the cake in approximately the same size space before beginning on the cake itself. The same tubes and techniques can be used to make simple outline figures of animals or faces for a child's cake. Cakes can be placed on a lazy Susan or mixer turntable for ease in turning while decorating.

Sugar molds can be made for a special touch on the decorated cake. Combine 4 cups of granulated sugar and 1 egg white. Pack the mixture into the mold firmly. Either turn the mixture out of the mold to dry or allow it to dry in the mold. Some molds, such as bells, should be hollowed out when the edges have become firm but the center of the mold is still soft. Be sure to leave a ⅛- to ¼-inch shell all around the mold.

Commercial mixes are available to make sugar and candy molds. There are also many plastic and metal molds on the market in a wide array of designs and colors, such as Mother Goose characters, animals, booties, cupids, and Santas. These can be arranged on the sides or top of cakes.

9. *Rose:* A. Use No. 124 rose tube and decorating frosting (stiff enough for petal to stand up), such as Royal Frosting. Put a small square of waxed or silicone paper on head of flower nail. Hold cone at 45° angle, narrow end of tube pointing up and slightly toward center of nail. Squeeze cone *while turning the nail* counterclockwise. Continue till there is a base 1½ inches high.

B. Start second dome on top (see first flower on row). With tube in same position, squeeze 3 slightly overlapping petals around top of dome to make the bud.

C. The next 5 petals go under the bud, standing out a little. For last row of petals, start at bottom of dome, turning tube to side so petals will stand out. Let roses dry 8 hours, peel off paper, and attach to cake.

Perky blossoms give a fresh, springtime look to a party cake. Vary the color of the frosting and center of the blossom to carry out the theme for a luncheon or a shower.

Decorating ideas: Both frosting and trimming are used to decorate a cake. Fancy designs fashioned with frosting can be made after careful study and practice. Until this art is mastered, simple designs, such as borders, can be piped on cakes for that special, personal touch.

Trimming may be purchased or created from household items and foods. Supermarkets and specialty shops carry a wide selection of dolls, animal figures, and holiday items to be used on top of and around cakes. Common, household items when combined with a little imagination make clever decorations. The following suggestions can be used to decorate a cake or combined with other ideas for different and original decorations.

Crisscross trim: Spread a creamy butter frosting over the cake. Cover top with parallel lines made by drawing tines of a fork through frosting. At right angles, draw fork through frosting again, leaving a one-half inch space between strokes.

Tinted coconut: Place shredded or flaked coconut in jar with few drops of desired food coloring. Cover jar; shake till all pieces are uniformly colored.

Coffee coconut: In a pint jar, mix 1½ teaspoons *each* of instant coffee powder and water. Add one 3½-ounce can flaked coconut. Cover jar and shake well. Spread on baking sheet; toast in 300° oven 20 minutes, stirring occasionally.

Cut marshmallow into 5 slices. Squeeze a point on each. Overlap and press petals together. Dot with a slice of red gumdrop.

Gumdrop bow: Between sheets of waxed paper, roll out two large gumdrops in long strips (have sugar on both sides of candy). Cut strips in half lengthwise and trim to ½ inch wide. Arrange loop of bow by bringing ends of 1 strip together. Place 2 loops on frosting. Place a small strip over center to cover "seam." Complete bow by adding 2 strips for streamers.

Gumdrop autumn leaves: Between sheets of waxed paper, roll out large gumdrops of fall colors. Cut with tiny leaf-shaped cutter or make leaf pattern of cardboard and cut around it with sharp knife.

Train cake: Bake cake in concentrated juice cans. Frost each cake, use round peppermint candies for the wheels, cut gumdrops in squares for windows, and link cars together for the train. The engine is made by placing a small square of cake on top of the first car. The caboose, of course, is bright red.

Halloween cake: Make a spider web by drizzling melted chocolate in circles on top of a frosted, round cake. Draw a knife lightly from the center to the edges of the cake for a web effect.

The art of cake decorating is not confined to cakes. The same techniques can be used on cookies, pastries, petits fours, and napoleans. Canapés are unusual with cream cheese piped on them. Salads and desserts can be garnished with whipped cream or cream cheese. (See also *Frosting.*)

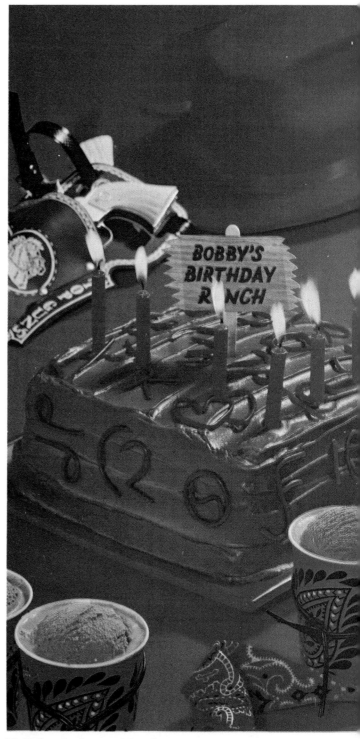

Delight the boys with a handsome birthday cake. Red and black licorice brands can be made using area ranch brands, favorite TV show brands, and the children's own initials.

Flexible licorice sticks are warmed slightly and tied around cups as lariats or shaped into brands for the cowboy cake decoration.

CALA—A yeast-raised, sweet-fried rice cake from New Orleans. The cake is a breakfast specialty and, until recently, was sold piping hot by the many street corner venders in the French Quarter.

CALAMONDIN—A small, loose-skinned orange with a sharp, tart flavor, that is native to the Philippines and is now grown in the United States. The fruit makes excellent marmalade. (See also *Orange*.)

CALCIUM—An inorganic mineral nutrient essential to the growth and maintenance of bones and teeth, to the proper clotting of the blood, and to the normal reactions of muscles and nerves. Need for calcium in the diet is the greatest in growing children and during pregnancy.

Milk is the richest food source of calcium and unless milk and milk products such as cheese are generously included in the day's diet, it is difficult to get enough of the mineral to maintain good health. Also, since vitamin D is necessary for the body to use calcium, milk products fortified with vitamin D assure the calcium will be used to advantage. Skim milk, though low in fat, contains all the calcium of whole milk. Green leafy vegetables contribute calcium to the diet, also.

Milk need not always be served as a plain white beverage. To delight children, flavorings or a few drops of food coloring may be stirred into the milk. Cream-style soups, puddings, and cheese dishes are ways to increase the amount of calcium consumed. (See also *Nutrition*.)

CALF'S FOOT JELLY—A natural aspic obtained by the long slow cooking of thoroughly cleaned calves' feet. The broth, strained and clarified, may be sweetened and flavored with spices, wine, or lemon peel before being allowed to gel. The gelatin contains some protein and is occasionally used as a food for convalescents.

CALLIE HAM, CALA HAM—A name sometimes given to smoked picnic, a cut which comes from the pork shoulder instead of the leg. Contrary to popular belief, callie ham is not ham at all although the flavoring and coloring are similar. The name is said to have originated in California and is an abbreviation for the state. (See *Picnic, Pork* for additional information.)

CALORIE—A unit designating the heat-producing or energy-producing value in food when burned in the body. Technically, one calorie is the amount of heat necessary to raise the temperature of one kilogram of water one degree centigrade. Scientists arrive at the number of calories in food by placing an accurately measured amount of the food in an oxygen-filled steel container which is surrounded by water. The food is then ignited by an electrical fuse. Because of the oxygen around the sample, it burns instantly and completely. The heat given off, as it burns, is measured by recording the rise in temperature of the water surrounding the container.

The energy-producing substances in food are protein, carbohydrate, and fat; thus the calories in a specific food depend upon the amounts of each present. Each gram of protein or carbohydrate supplies four calories; a gram of fat supplies nine calories. Translated into ounces, this means that there are 115 calories per ounce of protein or carbohydrate and 255 calories per ounce of fat consumed.

Today many people are concerned about counting calories and rightly so, for when more calories are consumed than the body can burn up, the extra calories are stored in the body as fatty tissue. Thus, the number of calories each person needs is related to his own energy requirements. The greater the energy expended in physical activity or growth, the more calories the body needs. Children and active teen-agers burn more calories for growth than adults.

As people pass childhood and have desk jobs or other sedentary occupations, fewer calories are necessary to maintain body weight. Nutritionists use the ideal weight at age 22 as the weight that should be maintained throughout life.

There are three steps to estimate the number of calories you need to maintain the desired body weight. First, estimate the desirable weight for height by consulting a reliable weight chart. Second, if you are a woman, multiply this weight by the number 16, and if you are a man, by 18. Finally, subtract 10 calories for each year of age over 22. (The estimate you arrive at is based on light amounts of physical activity. Additional calories are necessary if you regularly engage in strenuous activities. However, since many people tend to overestimate their energy requirements, this calculation will prove satisfactory for most of today's occupations.)

When fewer than this number of calories are consumed each day, there will be a steady weight loss. Likewise, extra calories bring about a weight gain.

Because the energy-producing aspect of food is only one area of good nutrition, any weight reduction or weight gaining program should be planned around a well-balanced diet and *should be supervised by a physician.* (See *Low-Calorie Cookery, Nutrition* for additional information.)

CAMBRIC TEA—A weak tea to which hot milk and sugar are added. It is prepared as a hot beverage for invalids or given to children as a substitute for full-strength brewed tea.

CAMEMBERT CHEESE (*kam' uhm bâr'*)—A ripened full flavored, French cheese. It has a golden to grayish outside rind and a light yellow interior. At its prime, it is waxy to semiliquid. Although the French export Camembert, varieties are also made in several other countries such as Germany and the United States.

Although a cheese of this type was known in Normandy for many years, credit for inventing Camembert cheese in the late 1700s goes to Mme. Marie Harel of Camembert, located just outside Vimoutiers. In fact, a monument to her honor stands near the farm where she lived.

The naming of the cheese is credited to the Emperor Napoleon who is said to have named the cheese after its place of origin during one of his visits to the district.

How Camembert is made: Whole milk is used in the production of this famous cheese. After the cheese has been drained from the whey, the curd is innoculated or a mold is sprayed on the surface. Next, the cheese is allowed to ripen from four to six weeks. As with many fine cheeses, geo-

graphic conditions and local customs influence the final product. Thus, American and French Camembert, while similar, will not be the same in flavor and texture.

Nutritional value: A one-ounce portion of Camembert cheese contains 84 calories. Some protein and small amounts of several vitamins and minerals are present.

How to select: Once, France was the best place to buy Camembert cheeses, but because shipping time and storage affect the cheese, some of the imported Camembert has passed its peak of quality by the time it reaches the consumer. Most authorities suggest avoiding imported Camembert in the summer months because it may be overripe. American cheese lovers are fortunate because domestic Camembert is somewhat more stable and does not have as far to travel. Generally, turnover in your store's refrigerated dairy case is frequent enough to assure getting good cheese. Remember that if the aroma of the Camem-

Toasty brown Camembert-Apple Sandwiches combine fruit and cheese in a hot entrée. Panned apple rings are the garnish.

bert cheese is strong when cold, this indicates that the cheese is past its prime. Whole cheeses weighing ten ounces are about 4½ inches in diameter. However, much of the Camembert cheese in United States markets is sold in individually wrapped triangles. (See also *Cheese*.)

Camembert-Apple Sandwich

4 1⅓-ounce triangles Camembert
   cheese
8 slices white bread
2 apples, peeled, cored, and sliced
   Lemon juice
   Butter or margarine
   Panned Apple Rings

Spread ½ triangle of cheese on each bread slice. Arrange apples over cheese on *four* of the slices; sprinkle lightly with lemon juice. Top each with one of the remaining bread slices, cheese side down. Spread butter on outside of sandwiches, top and bottom. Brown on both sides in skillet. Makes 4 servings. If desired, garnish with *Panned Apple Rings:* Core 1 apple and cut into four ½-inch slices. Cook in 1 tablespoon melted butter 5 to 6 minutes on each side.

CAMOMILE — A plant of the aster family whose fresh or dried flowers are brewed into an herb tea considered to have medicinal properties. The tea, sometimes called a tisane, was once popular as a mild tonic.

CAMPARI — An Italian red aperitif, flavored with bitter herbs. It is used in mixed drinks or along with a twist of lemon and soda. (See also *Wines and Spirits*.)

For dessert enjoy French Camembert cheese.

CAMPFIRE COOKERY — Preparing food over an open fire at a campsite and using a few cooking utensils brought from home or improvised on the spot. Since fire was first discovered, man has cooked his food over an open fire. However, today campfire cooking is usually limited to a single meal in a nearby park or a few days roughing it on a hunting or fishing trip. And much of the "roughing it" is eliminated when camping with car and trailer since there is space to carry more dishes and equipment. These, plus the new camp stoves and folding ovens, have taken over the major outdoor cooking.

A good cooking fire is essential for open-fire cooking. It is different from a bonfire because a cooking campfire needs to have steady, hot coals, and produce a minimum of smoke and flying sparks. The secret is to have a good bed of coals. Flames are useful only when you plan to use a reflector oven for baking or to boil water.

How to prepare breads: Use a reflector oven to bake muffins, pies, bread, biscuits, and cookies. This type of oven consists of a shelf set horizontally between two sloping metal surfaces. The heat of the fire is caught and reflected from the shiny metal shelf onto the top and bottom of the foods placed in the center of the shelf. For best baking results, make sure the fire is even, and place the oven so it gets the full benefit of the flames. By carefully maintaining the fire at about the same height and width as the oven, you will have constant heat during baking time.

Don't overlook packaged foods; they make outdoor baking an easy job. Also, a biscuit mix comes in handy for muffins and pancakes as well as for biscuits. Or, select one of the special mixes for coffee cakes, muffins, nut breads, cookies, cornbread, and gingerbread. Some even come complete with a baking pan. However, you

Campsite feast

Foods lose a rustic look when attractively → served. Rice-Mushroom Barbecue, cooked in foil, was transferred to serving bowl.

may prefer to pack ingredients for individual batches of biscuits in sealed plastic bags or containers. Add the liquid at the campsite. Bake the biscuits on ungreased foil or a baking sheet in a reflector oven.

Brown-and-serve rolls bake quickly in a reflector oven. For breakfast, simply brush rolls with melted butter, cut a slit in the tops, and spoon in strawberry jam or marmalade before placing these quick, sweet rolls on the oven shelf.

For those short camping trips, refrigerated biscuits will stay fresh in an ice chest and can be baked in a reflector oven. However, you can bake refrigerated biscuits in a lightly greased skillet over coals. Make sure you place the biscuits so they do not touch one another. Then cover and bake, turning biscuits once so that they brown both on the top and the bottom.

Bake bread twists made from biscuit dough on a stick directly over the coals. Add more liquid if needed to make dough easy to handle. Roll dough into foot-long strips. Wind a bread strip around center of sharpened, peeled, green stick, about two feet long and one to two inches in diameter. Be sure that the coils of dough do not touch. You can hold the sticks over the fire, but, it is easier to push sticks into ground at an angle to hold the twists of dough over coals. Keep turning the sticks as dough bakes. When twists are half done, lift the sticks out of the ground. Reverse them by pushing into the ground the end of stick that had been suspended over the fire; finish baking.

How to prepare fish: Serving freshly caught fish is one of the joys of a meal cooked out-of-doors. After cleaning the fish, remove the fins and tails if desired. Some campers skin their catch before cooking. You can cook the fish whole, or as steaks or fillets which fit the pan and assure uniform pieces.

Pan-ready fish can be dipped in either cornmeal or flour or a combination of the two. Heat bacon drippings or butter in a skillet and fry fish quickly. You can also cook fish in foil. Wrap the cleaned fish with a slice or two of bacon. This prevents sticking and adds flavor. Then fold the foil around the fish and place on the coals.

Don't overcook fish. It should be moist and tender with a delicate flavor. Overcooking causes it to become increasingly dry and chewy. The fish is done when its flesh is translucent and flakes easily with a fork.

You can plank and cook a large fish weighing several pounds before an open fire. Remove the tail and head, then split the fish along the back but do not cut all the way through. Lay the fish out flat; then rub butter and salt into the fish before you tack it to a board or split log with hardwood slivers. Prop up the log or board before a high fire to cook.

How to prepare meats and main dishes: When camping, make use of a skillet, grill, grill basket, or foil wrap for most of your meat cookery. Simply follow the same principles as for barbecuing. You may prefer steaks that have been grilled right on the hot coals, as some lovers of the out-of-doors do. This requires a level bed of hardwood embers which should measure at least twice as large as the meat being grilled. Place the thick-cut steaks directly on the hot coals which are made ash-free by tapping or blowing away the white ashes. As the drippings hit the fire, flames leap up, imparting a good char flavor. Turn the meat frequently. This keeps it juicy and avoids burning the meat. Each time you turn the steak, it should land on fresh coals. Steaks cooked on the coals will be rare inside even though they are charred black on the outside.

If you're like most campers, bacon is not only a favorite food but also a versatile one. It can be threaded on a sharpened stick and held over the coals, fried in a skillet, or grilled on a piece of heavy foil with edges turned up to form a pan. And the drippings can be saved.

Grill-cooked hamburgers are always popular in camp. Place the patties on the grill as in barbecuing, or cook on a piece of heavy foil which is punctured at intervals. If the hamburgers are individually wrapped in heavy foil, there's no need to blow ash off the coals before adding the foil-wrapped burgers. The ash helps protect foil from extreme heat. Make burgers thick if they are to be served rare; thinner if well-done meat is preferred.

Many campsite meals are built around meat and vegetable combinations. Some are cooked in a heavy skillet or large kettle. Others are baked in foil on the coals.

Campsite Stew

In skillet brown 1 pound ground beef and ½ cup chopped onion. Add one 10½-ounce can condensed beef broth; one 16-ounce can cream-style corn; 3 large potatoes, peeled and diced; 1 teaspoon salt; and dash pepper. Cover; cook over *medium* coals 20 to 45 minutes. Stir occasionally. Makes 4 generous servings.

Campfire Spaghetti

    2 15-ounce cans barbecue sauce
      and beef
    1 18-ounce can tomato juice
      (2¼ cups)
    2 tablespoons instant minced onion
    1 teaspoon dried oregano leaves,
      crushed
    1 7-ounce package uncooked
      spaghetti
      Parmesan cheese

Combine first 4 ingredients and 2 cups water in large kettle. Cover and bring to boiling over *medium* coals. Add spaghetti; stir to separate strands. Simmer, covered, 20 to 25 minutes or till spaghetti is tender. Stir frequently. Add water if needed to prevent sticking. Pass Parmesan cheese. Makes 6 servings.

Sausage-Apple Wrap

Shape 1 pound bulk pork sausage into 4 patties, ½-inch thick. Place each patty on a 12-inch square of heavy foil. Peel, core, and slice 2 medium apples. Arrange apple slices spoke fashion atop patties. Blend 3 tablespoons sugar with ½ teaspoon ground cinnamon; sprinkle over apples. Spoon contents of one 8-ounce can whole cranberry sauce over apples. Draw up four corners of foil to center and twist to secure, allowing room for expansion of steam. Bake over *medium* coals for 20 to 25 minutes or till the sausage is done and the apples are tender. Makes 4 servings.

Other foods to prepare: Good campfire coffee is a must and not difficult to make. Many campers carry instant coffee because it takes so little space to pack. However, real campfire coffee has no equal. First measure the water by adding the number of cups needed, plus a little extra to make up for the water that will boil away. Then bring to a hard, rolling boil. Allow a rounded tablespoonful of coffee for every cup of water used, then add one additional spoonful.

Boil to the desired strength; set off coals, but keep them close enough so coffee will stay hot; add a little cold water, if desired; coffee will settle in a few minutes. For clearer coffee, mix egg and shell with dry grounds before adding to boiling water.

Many campers bake potatoes in foil; however, clean, empty soup-size cans are handy, too. Be sure the scrubbed potatoes have been pricked to allow for steam to escape. Cover open ends of cans with foil. Lay cans on grill or on coals; roll occasionally during baking. Some campers place potatoes right in the coals without foil or cans. The skins burn black but the insides are white and delicious.

Packaged, precooked rice is another good camping staple. It can be cooked in a skillet or conveniently wrapped in a foil packet. (See also *Barbecue*.)

Rice-Mushroom Barbecue

    1⅓ cups uncooked package precooked
        rice
      1 3-ounce can sliced mushrooms
    ¼ cup finely chopped onion
      1 teaspoon Worcestershire sauce
    ½ teaspoon salt
      2 tablespoons butter or margarine

Tear off a 3-foot length of wide heavy foil; fold in half to make a square. Form foil into a pouch. Add uncooked rice, *undrained* mushrooms, 1 cup cold water, onion, Worcestershire sauce, and salt. Stir carefully to mix. Dot top with butter. Fold edges of foil to seal pouch tightly. Place on grill over *hot* coals for 15 to 18 minutes. Before serving, open foil and add an extra pat of butter; gently fluff the rice with a fork. Makes 4 servings.

CANADIAN COOKERY—A wide range of food-preparation techniques and dishes that are influenced by the geography of Canada and the nationality of its settlers. Canada is vast and stretches the width of the North American continent and up past the Arctic Circle. Within its boundaries are rocky seacoasts, bountiful central plains, towering mountains, and the rugged territory of the Yukon.

Canada is a melting pot of nationalities, too. English, Scottish, and French settlers have been joined over the years by families from Germany, Ireland, Central Europe and Scandinavia, from the Orient, Poland, and Russia. Over a large part of the country, the cooking is similar to that of the United States. But, each nationality group has added its traditional recipes or adapted them to the plenty of the land and sea. Three meals a day, usually relatively heavy, are the general rule. And the British touch of afternoon tea is often evident.

The cookery of the eastern provinces shows a number of influences. Some of the fishing towns in Nova Scotia are typical. They were founded in the mid-eighteenth century by Hanoverian "Dutch" settlers. The settlers came mainly from farmlands, but became fishermen as they established a prosperous fishing industry. The influence of the sea is noted in many dishes popular to the area, such as fried cod cheeks and tongues, salt cod with potatoes, boiled mackerel in sauce, and baked haddock or halibut.

Even though seafood became an important part of daily meals, the handed-down recipes from the homeland survive in daily use. There are yeasty barley breads, hearty noodle soups, cucumber or leaf lettuce in sour cream sauce, raised doughnuts and stollen, and sauerkraut or turnip kraut served in a dozen ways. English neighbors introduced scones, finnan haddie, shortbread, trifle pudding, and corned beef served with cabbage.

The Gaspé Peninsula, jutting out from the east coast, is famous for its salmon. But the basic, simple meat and vegetable dishes, that make up most of the daily meals on the north side of the Peninsula, show strong influence of provincial French cooking. The south side of the Peninsula, largely populated by descendants of Scottish and English settlers reflects the cooking style of Great Britain.

In Quebec, the metropolitan heart of the eastern provinces, and to some extent in Montreal, French cookery predominates. Here a stew is a ragout, and many dishes are prepared *à la Canadienne*. French recipes and techniques have been adapted to foods plentiful in Canada. Hearty, satisfying, dried pea soup is a staple food. Twisted, light and airy French crullers are popular. Meats are roasted or braised in the French style with herbs and spices. Here is found thick, creamy cheese soup, delectable *Tourtière*, a two-crust meat pie of pork or pork and veal.

Tourtière (Canadian Pork Pie)

> 1 pound lean ground pork
> 1 cup water
> ½ cup finely chopped onion
> ½ cup fine dry bread crumbs
> ¾ teaspoon salt
>   Dash pepper
>   Dash ground sage
>   Dash ground nutmeg
>   Plain Pastry for 2-crust 9-inch pie
>   (See *Pastry*)

Brown pork in skillet; drain off excess fat. Add remaining ingredients *except* pastry. Simmer covered 30 minutes, stirring occasionally. Line 9-inch pie plate with *half* of pastry. Turn meat mixture into crust. Adjust top crust; seal. Cut slits in top to permit escape of steam. Bake at 400° for 35 minutes or till crust is a deep golden brown. Makes 6 servings.

English and Scottish influence is strong in most of the rest of Canada. Breakfast is a hearty meal. A "joint" or roast is much favored as the basis for dinner, with roast beef and Yorkshire pudding prominent. Steak and kidney pie is a standby. Porridge and other Scottish favorites are often listed on the restaurant menus.

Where Italian families live, traditional Italian cookery predominates. Where Russians, Ukrainians, and Polish have settled in the West and Northwest regions, there is a distinct Slavic influence. Dumplings, stuffed cabbage, borscht, and meats in sour cream sauce such as beef stroganoff are popular. Scandinavians prepare their national dishes, too. In the Far West, Vancouver, a melting-pot city, has a polyglot population. The typical foods of many nationalities are enjoyed, and this is where Chinese foods can also be found. The seafood of this area is excellent, too.

Locally-produced foods find their way to the table in all sections of Canada. The great fruit-growing areas in Ontario and the West provide fresh and canned peaches, apricots, cherries, apples, and pears. Excellent Canadian cheeses including blues and Cheddars are used generously as a separate course or in cooking. The abundant maple syrup is popular throughout the country in such dishes as the French maple syrup pie, in custards, and both on and in hot breads and cakes.

Maple Syrup Pie

½ cup cold water
3 tablespoons cornstarch
1 cup maple syrup

. . .

1 tablespoon butter or margarine
Plain Pastry for 2-crust 8-inch pie
(See *Pastry*)
½ cup chopped walnuts

In medium saucepan, blend cold water into cornstarch. Add maple syrup. Cook and stir over medium heat till mixture is thick and bubbly; cook 1 minute more. Add butter; pour into pastry-lined pie plate. Sprinkle with nuts. Cover with top crust; seal and flute edges. Bake pie at 400° till pastry is golden brown. This requires about 30 minutes.

Though many kinds of furred and feathered game are cooked and served throughout Canada, the great Northwest is the area where they abound. Fish, including Pacific salmon, are plentiful. Bear, bison, caribou, and moose are made into delicious roasts and stews. Wild birds are in abundance and so is the wild rice so good to serve with them.

CANADIAN-STYLE BACON—Boned pork loin that has been cured and smoked. In Canada it is known as back bacon. Before it was produced in the United States, meat packers imported this bacon and called it Canadian bacon. After United States production started, government regulations required the word "style" be added.

Since it is made from a large, lean muscle, Canadian-style bacon has less fat than regular bacon. A single slice, cut ¼ inch thick, contains 65 calories. It is an excellent source of high-quality meat protein and of the B vitamin, thiamine.

Both the cook-before-eating and the fully cooked Canadian-style bacon are available. The slices panfry or heat quickly for breakfast, sandwiches, or main dishes. When purchased by the piece, it may be baked in the oven or cooked on a rotisserie.

Roast Canadian Bacon

2½ pounds fully-cooked Canadian-style bacon

. . .

½ cup currant jelly
1 teaspoon dry mustard
¼ teaspoon finely grated orange peel

Remove outer wrap from bacon. Score in 1½-inch squares, cutting about ¼ inch deep. Adjust on spit; roast over *medium hot* coals. Have foil pan under bacon. Blend remaining ingredients for glaze. Broil about 1 hour and 15 minutes; brush with glaze during last 10 to 15 minutes. Slice and serve. Serves 10 to 12.

Canadian Bacon-Bean Bake

Combine one 16-ounce can pork and beans in tomato sauce with 1 tablespoon instant minced onion, ¼ cup catsup, 2 teaspoons *each* prepared horseradish and prepared mustard, and 1 teaspoon Worcestershire sauce. Pour into a 10x6x1½-inch baking dish. Bake at 350° for 45 minutes. Arrange four ¼-inch-thick orange slices and eight ¼-inch-thick Canadian-style bacon slices, on top. Sprinkle with ⅓ cup brown sugar; dot with 2 tablespoons butter. Bake for 30 minutes more. Makes 4 servings.

CANAPÉ *(kan' uh pē, kan' uh pā')*—An appetizer with an edible base that is usually eaten with the fingers. It is served hot or cold as a cocktail accompaniment.

The traditional base for a canapé is a thin piece of bread. Remove the bread crusts and cut the bread into neat shapes with sharp cutters or a knife, then toast. You can spread the base with flavored butters, or meat, fish, cheese, or fruit spreads. The topping can be as elaborate as caviar, smoked salmon, lobster, or a pâté, or as simple as melted cheese or a crisp cucumber slice. Other bases that you can use for canapés are thin pastry cutouts, and thin crackers or wafers. Melba toast also makes a good choice as a canapé base.

Garnishes for the top of these tiny sandwiches can be capers, truffles, mushrooms, sieved egg, watercress, parsley, olive slices, pimiento pieces, or pickles.

The charm of canapés is not only in their good taste but in their freshly made (not soggy) texture, and dainty appearance.

Canapés can be very time-consuming, so to avoid last minute preparation, prepare cold canapés ahead of time. Chill them before serving for best results. Even some hot canapés can be partially prepared ahead of time. Once fixed, these appetizers can be popped under the broiler just before serving. (See also *Appetizer*.)

Tiny, bite-sized Kabob Canapés can be served for a spur-of-the-moment cocktail party since they are simply made.

Crab Meat-Bacon Rounds

    2 egg whites
    2 ounces sharp Cheddar cheese,
       shredded (½ cup)
    1 7½-ounce can crab meat, drained
       flaked, and cartilage removed
   20 2-inch toast rounds, buttered
    3 slices bacon, finely diced
       Pimiento-stuffed green olives,
       sliced

Beat egg whites till stiff peaks form. Fold shredded cheese and drained crab meat into egg whites. Pile crab meat mixture on buttered toast rounds. Partially cook the bacon; sprinkle on top of crab mixture. Broil till cheese starts to melt and bacon is crisp. Top each canapé with an olive slice. Makes 20 canapés.

Hot Steak Canapés

Have beef strip sirloin steak or whole tenderloin sliced 1½ to 2 inches thick. Broil 2 to 4 inches from heat to desired doneness. Season with salt and pepper. Slice thin and serve hot on thin slices of salty rye bread.

Ham and Rye Rounds

Score one 3-pound canned ham in 1-inch diamonds. Combine ½ cup brown sugar, ¼ cup dark corn syrup, and 1 tablespoon fruit juice. Heat till sugar dissolves. Bake ham at 350° for 45 minutes, glazing 4 times with sugar mixture.

Whip ½ cup butter with 2 tablespoons prepared mustard till fluffy. Spread on slices of party rye bread; serve with thin ham slices.

Kabob Canapés

Slice one 12-ounce can luncheon meat. With tiny cutters, cut meat into fancy shapes. Cut out same shapes from bread, making two for each meat cutout. Butter one side of bread.

Dip meat in catsup. Place meat on unbuttered side of bread cutout. Top each with another bread cutout, buttered side up. Broil both sides of "sandwich" to toast bread. To serve, skewer with wooden picks and top each with a pimiento-stuffed green olive.

These tasty canapés require some last-minute preparation. Swiss Sandwich Puffs are at their best piping hot from the broiler.

Ham Chippers

½ cup crushed potato chips
Plain Pastry for 1-crust 9-inch pie (See *Pastry*)
1 4½-ounce can deviled ham
2 tablespoons dry sherry
1 tablespoon chopped canned pimiento
Chopped pecans

Spread crushed potato chips on well-floured surface; roll pastry out over chips, about ⅛ inch thick. Cut into 2¼-inch rounds. Fit into about twenty-four 1½-inch muffin cups. Prick each with fork. Chill the pastry shells at least 15 minutes. (Unbaked shells will keep in refrigerator for several hours.)

To serve, bake at 425° for 10 minutes or till golden brown. Combine ham, sherry, and pimiento. Heat just to boiling. Spoon into shells. Garnish with chopped pecans. Serve warm. Makes about 24 canapés.

Swiss Sandwich Puffs

½ cup mayonnaise
¼ cup chopped onion
2 tablespoons snipped parsley
32 tiny rye slices, toasted
8 slices Swiss cheese, quartered

Combine mayonnaise, onion, and parsley. Spread on toasted rye bread. Top each with a ¼ slice of cheese. Place under broiler 2 to 3 minutes to melt cheese. Makes 32 canapés.

Hot Chicken Spread

2 cups coarsely ground cooked chicken
½ cup ground almonds
½ cup mayonnaise or salad dressing
¼ teaspoon curry powder
Assorted crackers, melba toast rounds, or potato chips
Paprika

Blend first 4 ingredients. Add salt to taste. Spread on crackers, toast, or chips. Sprinkle with paprika. Place on baking sheet. Bake at 400° for 3 minutes. Makes 2 cups.

Lobster Canapés

Cut thirty 2-inch bread rounds from thinly sliced bread. Brush lightly with salad oil. Heat at 225° for 1¼ to 1½ hours or till crisp.

Shred one 5-ounce can lobster. Combine with ½ cup canned condensed cream of mushroom soup, 2 tablespoons dry white wine, 1 tablespoon chopped canned pimiento, ¼ teaspoon salt, and few drops bottled hot pepper sauce. Spread mixture on toasted bread. Sprinkle with ¼ cup buttered fine dry bread crumbs. Broil 2 to 3 minutes. Makes 30 canapés.

Dried Beef Canapés

Cook 1 teaspoon finely chopped onion in 1 tablespoon butter till tender but not brown. Add one 2½-ounce jar sliced dried beef, finely chopped. Cook till beef is slightly crisp. Add beef mixture to one 3-ounce package cream cheese. Blend well. Spread on crisp rye wafers.

CANARD *(kuh närd')*—The French word for duck. A famous dish is *Canard à la Presse*, (pressed duck). It's prepared using rare duck and incorporating the duck blood. A special press is used and preparation is usually done at the table. (See also *Duck.*)

CANDIED FLOWER—A flower which is candied or crystallized for use as an especially elegant garnish on desserts. Some flowers, such as candied violets, are imported from France. Others can be prepared using garden or greenhouse flowers.

Beat 1 egg white slightly in a small dish. Stir in 1 tablespoon water. Brush egg white mixture on petals of flowers with brush.

Sprinkle granulated sugar on flowers that have been brushed with egg white. Place on cooling rack till sugar coating is dry.

For a festive touch, decorate a heart-shaped cake with a colorful nosegay of assorted candied or crystallized flowers.

First, choose small flowers for candying, such as tiny roses, carnations, or bachelor buttons. Brush with egg white mixture, then sprinkle with sugar. Let dry on rack. If not used immediately, store in a dry place.

Frost the cake with fluffy frosting. Prepare the nosegay by clipping stems closely. Insert flowers in a large dollop of frosting in center of doily. Place doily on cake.

CANDIED FRUIT AND PEEL

CANDIED FRUIT AND PEEL — Syrup-saturated fruit and peel used as an ingredient in fruitcake and other baked foods. It is also used as a decoration for cakes, particularly at holiday time, and for eating out-of-hand. By preparing it in the sugar syrup, it helps preserve the food and enhances the flavor. Among the many types available are candied citron, orange peel, grapefruit peel, lemon peel, pineapple slices, and candied red and green cherries.

Most of the candying done in the United States is with citrus peel. Other candied fruits and peels are imported from Italy and France. Whole pieces of candied fruit are also available in some markets. Uniformly diced fruits are packaged separately as well as in mixtures suitable for fruitcakes. Citrus peel, cut in strips, is easily candied in the home kitchen and is usually served as a confection.

Store candied fruit and peel in tightly covered containers.

Basic Fruit Dough

        2 packages active dry yeast
        2 cups sifted all-purpose flour
        ¾ cup pineapple juice
        ½ cup shortening
        ⅓ cup sugar
        2 eggs
        2 teaspoons grated lemon peel
        ¾ cup light raisins
        ½ cup chopped candied pineapple
     2½ to 3 cups sifted all-purpose
            flour

In large mixer bowl combine yeast and 2 cups sifted flour. In saucepan combine pineapple juice, ½ cup water, shortening, sugar, and 1½ teaspoons salt. Heat just till warm, stirring occasionally to melt the shortening. Add to dry mixture in mixing bowl. Add eggs and lemon peel. Beat at low speed with electric mixer for ½ minute, scraping sides of bowl constantly. Beat 3 minutes at high speed.

Stir in raisins and pineapple. By hand stir in enough of the 2½ to 3 cups flour to make a soft to moderately stiff dough.

Turn out on lightly floured surface. Knead till smooth, about 10 minutes. Place in greased bowl; turn once to grease surface. Cover; let rise in warm place till doubled, 1 to 1½ hours. Punch down; let rest 10 minutes. Shape dough in one of the following ways:

Crown Coffee Bread

Using Basic Fruit Dough, pat ¾ of dough evenly into a greased 10-inch tube pan. Divide remaining dough in half; roll each to 28-inch strand. Twist together. Place on top of dough; seal ends. Cover; let rise till doubled, 45 to 60 minutes. Bake at 375° about 45 minutes. Brush with butter and sprinkle lightly with granulated sugar. Makes 1 large loaf.

Topknot Loaves

Using Basic Fruit Dough, divide dough in fourths. Pat into 4 well-greased 16-ounce cans; smooth tops. Cover; let rise till dough is about 1-inch above top of can, 30 to 45 minutes. Bake at 375° about 40 minutes. Remove from cans; cool. Frost with Confectioners' Sugar Icing; top with nuts. Makes 4 loaves.

Petal Bread

Using Basic Fruit Dough, divide dough in thirds. Shape each into a smooth ball. Place balls on lightly greased baking sheet with balls just touching. Cover and let rise till doubled, about 45 minutes. Bake at 350° about 35 minutes. Cool. Prepare *Confectioners' Sugar Icing:* Combine ¾ cup sifted confectioners' sugar and 1 tablespoon milk; beat till smooth. Spread over bread. Trim with almonds and candied cherries. Makes one 3-part loaf.

Fruit Rolls

Using Basic Fruit Dough, turn dough out on lightly floured surface. Roll to ½ inch thick. Cut with 2½-inch biscuit cutter and shape in rolls. Place on greased baking sheet. Cover; let rise till almost doubled, about 45 minutes. Cut shallow cross in each roll with sharp knife. Brush tops with 1 slightly beaten egg white. Bake at 375° about 15 minutes. Cool slightly. Mark crosses on rolls with Confectioners' Sugar Icing. Makes 2 dozen rolls

Candied Grapefruit Peel comes in three colors. To make this confection extra fancy, cut peel with small cookie cutters, then roll in giant-size sugar crystals or colored sugar.

Candied Grapefruit Peel

    2 medium grapefruit
1½ cups sugar
  ¾ cup water
    1 3-ounce package lemon-, lime-, or
      strawberry-flavored gelatin
    Sugar

Score grapefruit peel in 4 lengthwise sections with point of knife. Loosen from pulp with bowl of spoon. Remove most of the white membrane from peel. Cut peel into ¼-inch strips or various shapes with cookie cutters.

Place 2 cups of cut peel in large pan. Cover completely with cold water. Boil 20 minutes. Drain. Repeat process twice with fresh water each time. Drain thoroughly.

Combine 1½ cups sugar, water, and ¼ teaspoon salt in 2-quart saucepan. Cook and stir to dissolve sugar. Add peel; bring to boiling. Simmer 20 minutes or till peel is just translucent. Gradually add flavored gelatin, stirring over low heat till gelatin is dissolved.

Remove peel from syrup; drain on rack. Let stand 20 minutes. Roll each piece in granulated or colored sugar. Let dry on rack several hours. Store in a covered jar.

Candied Orange Peel

>   6 medium oranges
>   1 tablespoon salt
>   4 cups water
>   2 cups sugar
>   ½ cup water
>   Sugar

Cut peel of each orange in sixths; loosen from pulp with bowl of spoon. Remove most of white membrane from peel. Add salt and peel to 4 cups water. Weight with a plate to keep peel under water; let stand overnight. Drain; rinse thoroughly. Cover with cold water; heat to boiling. Drain. Repeat this process 3 times to help remove the bitter taste.

With shears, cut peel in strips. In saucepan combine peel (about 2 cups), 2 cups sugar, and ½ cup water. Heat and stir till sugar dissolves. Cook slowly till peel is translucent. Drain; roll in sugar. Dry on rack. Store in a covered jar. Makes 2 to 2½ cups peel.

No-Bake Fruit Squares

>   1 cup raisins
>   1 cup pitted dates
>   ½ cup dried apricots
>   ½ cup candied orange peel
>   ⅓ cup dried figs
>   ¼ cup candied cherries
>   1 cup chopped walnuts
>   2 to 3 tablespoons orange juice
>   Confectioners' sugar

Grind together raisins, dates, dried apricots, candied orange peel, dried figs, candied cherries, and walnuts. Mix in enough of the orange juice to hold mixture together. Press into greased 8x8x2-inch pan. Chill several hours or overnight. Cut into squares; sift confectioners' sugar atop. Makes about 36.

CANDIED GINGER—Sugar-saturated ginger that is used as a confection or as an ingredient, also called crystallized ginger. It has visible sugar crystals coating the pieces and is usually packed in boxes.

Preserved ginger is also a type of candied ginger that is purchased in jars and is packed in a syrup. (See also *Ginger*.)

Oriental Fruit Freeze

Blend together one 3-ounce package cream cheese, softened; ¼ cup mayonnaise; and 1 tablespoon lemon juice. Drain one 11-ounce can mandarin oranges; cut up oranges. Stir oranges, ½ cup chopped dates, ¼ cup quartered maraschino cherries, and 1 tablespoon finely chopped candied ginger into cheese mixture.

Whip 1 cup whipping cream. Fold into fruit-cheese mixture. Pour into freezer tray and sprinkle ¼ cup slivered almonds, toasted, over top. Freeze till firm. Remove from freezer 10 minutes before serving. Serves 6 to 8.

CANDIED VEGETABLE—A vegetable that has been glazed with a sweet, sugar-type mixture. Vegetables that are often candied are sweet potatoes, acorn squash, carrots, and beets. (See also *Vegetable*.)

Candied Carrots

>   5 medium carrots
>   ¼ cup butter or margarine
>   ¼ cup canned jellied cranberry
>   sauce
>   2 tablespoons brown sugar
>   ½ teaspoon salt

Slice carrots crosswise on the bias, about ½ inch thick. In a saucepan cook carrots, covered, in small amount of boiling salted water till just tender, about 6 to 10 minutes.

In a skillet combine remaining ingredients. Heat slowly and stir till cranberry sauce melts. Add drained carrots; heat, stirring occasionally, till nicely glazed on all sides, about 5 minutes. Makes 4 servings.

Candied Beets

Drain one 16-ounce can sliced beets, *reserving 2 tablespoons liquid*. In saucepan combine the drained beets, reserved liquid, ¼ cup currant jelly, 2 tablespoons vinegar, dash salt, and dash ground cloves. Cover and simmer 10 minutes. Mix 1 teaspoon cornstarch and 1 teaspoon cold water; stir into beet mixture. Cook and stir till mixture thickens and bubbles. Add 1 tablespoon butter. Makes 4 servings.

CANDY

*Tips for making, storing, and mailing candy
that will satisfy even the sweetest tooth.*

Candy is a confection or sweet using sugar, or an ingredient high in sugar, as the basic ingredient. Often flavorings, such as chocolate, fruits, and nuts are added. Homemade candy is a joy to make, serve, and give to friends, particularly at holiday time. And it's not difficult to make if all steps in the recipe are followed exactly and if an understanding of the different types of candies is mastered.

No one really knows who first enjoyed the delight of a sugar-sweet piece of candy. But about 4,000 years ago, the Egyptians had established the art of making confectionery. They honored this achievement by showing the candy making process in drawings on the walls of temples and tombs. Their candy used honey as the sweetener, because sugar refining was unknown at the time. Spices and herbs were used as flavorings and coloring was added.

Ancient Persians made a delicacy from a sweet-tasting reed plus honey and spices. They called it *kand.* Their Arab neighbors, after learning to use sugar cane, contrived a sugar refining process and made lozenges of fine sugar and gum arabic. This sugar refining process was one of the greatest contributions to candy making. The Arabian word for sugar is "quand." Our word candy is said to be derived from the words kand and quand.

Besides serving as a sweet, another early use of candy was to hide the taste of unpleasant medicines.

Candy makes an ideal Chistmas gift

← Give a tin of Santa's Fudge, Cherry Divinity, red and green Crystal-Cut Candies, and Spicy Walnuts. (See *Walnut* for recipe.)

As sugar became popular over the globe, candy became a treat more widely available. Candy making developed into an art in Europe and this knowledge was brought to America. The town druggist was usually responsible for selling the professionally made candy, although candy was also being made in the home. The Indians taught early colonists how to use maple sugar in candies and how to flavor them with herbs.

Up to the mid-nineteenth century, most of the candy was made on a small scale. But commercial candy manufacturing in the United States started around 1850 when equipment was invented to improve the production of candy.

The candy bar was developed in the early 1900s. Later, with the improved manufacturing methods during World War I, candy bars were mass produced for the servicemen for quick energy. Now, a third of the United States candy market is in the familiar form of candy bars.

Nutritional value: The largest contribution that candy adds to the diet is in its energy or caloric content. Because sugar is such a good energy producer, candy can be that needed pick-me-up to relieve fatigue, especially during times of strenuous activity. The energy that a small piece of candy yields is high in proportion to its size and it is quickly usable in our bodies.

Sugar, as such, has no protein, vitamins, or minerals but does add calories to the diet. Sweets can dull the appetite if eaten before the meal, but they will give a satisfied feeling at the end of a meal. This is why sweet foods are usually eaten for dessert. Candy can add to the nutrition of the body if it is made with milk, dried cereals, nuts, or fruit, but this varies with the ingredients that are added.

Basic ingredients: The secret of good candy making is to bring about the formation of the right kind of crystals or to prevent the formation of any crystals at all. The kind and proportion of ingredients, the temperature to which the candy syrup is cooked, and the handling of the syrup after cooking is completed are influential factors in making good candy. And as in other cooking, it is very important to measure the ingredients accurately so that they will be in proper proportion to each other.

Granulated sugar is the basic candy ingredient. When a syrup of just sugar and water is concentrated by boiling, it crystallizes when cool to a hard, grainy solid. So, other ingredients are added to the sugar, not only for flavor, but to control or prevent crystallization.

Corn syrup, for example, in various proportions to the amount of sugar in the recipe, helps control crystal formation to make a creamy, or soft, chewy candy.

Acids, such as vinegar, cream of tartar, and lemon juice can be used to slow down crystallization. But even the least bit too much of any of these could prevent the formation of a desirable number of crystals, thus causing a runny product.

Butter and the fat in chocolate and milk, also slow down crystallization as well as add flavor to the candy.

Flavoring, such as vanilla, and nuts are added after the candy is cooked, during the beating of the mixture. If the candy is not beaten, flavorings are then added after removing the pan from heat.

Basic equipment: Choose a saucepan that is large enough to let the candy boil without bubbling over. It should be a fairly heavy saucepan that has a cover. A heavy saucepan helps keep candy from sticking to the bottom and scorching, and the cover is often used at the beginning of the cooking so that unwanted sugar crystals are steamed down into the mixture.

A candy thermometer is almost an indispensable item for candy making because it takes guesswork out of testing.

Use wooden spoons for beating and stirring since they never get too hot to handle. Wooden spoons also cut down on the noise when beating in a metal pan.

Basic cooking principles: Since controlled formation of crystals is so important to successful candy making, there are several techniques that will lead to success.

Stir the candy mixture until it comes to a boil. This assures you that the sugar is completely dissolved.

Because one sugar crystal attracts other crystals, clusters will form on the sides of the saucepan as the syrup cooks. You can prevent these unwanted crystals by covering the pan during the first few minutes of boiling. This lets the steam that is formed wash down any crystals that might cling. Or, recipes will often call for buttering the sides of the saucepan before adding other ingredients. If the recipe says to stir as it is being cooked, do so gently to avoid splashing syrup on sides of pan.

When milk is an ingredient in the recipe, cook over medium heat to avoid scorching the mixture. Candies made with water can be cooked over a higher heat.

Cooking candy to the correct temperature is a very critical part of candy making. To test the candy to see if it is "done," use a candy thermometer. This is probably the most accurate method of measuring. However, check the accuracy of the thermometer in boiling water each time it is used. If the thermometer registers above or below 212° (the boiling point of water), add or subtract degrees to make the same allowance in the recipe.

Be sure that the bulb of the thermometer is completely covered with boiling liquid, not just the foam, for an accurate reading. However, the bulb must not touch the bottom of the pan. Clip thermometer to pan after the syrup begins to boil. Be sure to watch gauge closely during last few minutes of cooking, because the temperature will rise quickly after 220°.

If a candy thermometer is not available, use the cold water test. To make this test, remove pan of candy from heat and immediately drop a few drops of boiling syrup from spoon into a cup of very cold (but not icy cold) water. Use fresh water and a clean spoon for each test. Form drops into a ball with fingers. The firmness of the ball indicates the temperature of the syrup. If the right stage has not been reached, quickly return pan to heat.

Remove pan and retest candy about every 2 to 3 minutes, or till desired stage is reached. See the temperatures and tests chart below for comparisons of tests.

Humidity affects the cooking of candy. If it's a rainy or very humid day, it's recommended that candies be cooked a degree or so above what is given in recipe.

High altitudes also affect the cooking of candy. Cook the syrup one degree lower than the temperature at sea level for each increase of 500 feet in elevation. For example, at soft-ball stage, the temperature range at sea level is 234° to 240°. At 2,000 feet the range for soft-ball stage would be 230° to 236°; at 5,000 feet the range is 224° to 230°; at 7,500 feet the range would be 219° to 225°.

How to store: Fudge and fondant will keep fresh and creamy for several weeks if tightly wrapped in waxed paper, foil, or clear plastic wrap. Many people think these are improved when stored. Store in an airtight container in a cool, dry place.

Taffies and caramels, or chewy candies, should be individually wrapped to keep out the moisture and to prevent them from becoming sticky. Store in an airtight container in a cool, dry place. Brittles should also be protected from dampness.

Keep chocolate-dipped candies in bon-bon cups and store in a cool, dry place.

Divinity is not a good keeper because it dries out quickly. So, eat while fresh!

Homemade and commercially made candies freeze well. Wrap candy box with foil or clear plastic wrap to protect candy.

Popcorn balls made with a candy syrup also freeze well. Wrap each separately in clear plastic wrap, then freeze in polyethylene bags till ready to use.

How to mail. Candy is a welcome gift that can easily be mailed. Choose candies that travel well, such as fudge, taffy, caramels, candied fruits, and fondant. Avoid such candies as brittles and divinity. Brittles will break too easily going through the mail, and divinity does not keep well.

To keep candy pieces neatly separated, wrap them individually or place in fluted paper cups. Then arrange the pieces of candy in a sturdy cardboard or metal container that is lined with waxed paper or attractive, lacy paper doilies.

Pack heavier candy on the bottom and more delicate types on top. Place plenty of crushed paper on top and bottom of candy and fill in the corners with paper. Tape box closed and print name and destination plainly on the package.

Temperatures and tests for candy

Temperatures (at Sea Level)	Stage	Cold-water Test
230° to 234°F	Thread	Syrup dropped from spoon spins 2-inch thread.
234° to 240°F	Soft ball	Syrup can be shaped into a ball but flattens when removed from water.
244° to 248°F	Firm ball	Syrup can be shaped into a firm ball which does not flatten when removed from water.
250° to 266°F	Hard ball	Syrup forms hard ball, although it is pliable.
270° to 290°F	Soft crack	Syrup separates into threads that are not brittle.
300° to 310°F	Hard crack	Syrup separates into hard, brittle threads.

Crystalline candy

Crystalline or creamy candies are one type of candy. In this group, the sugar dissolves completely and then, under certain conditions, crystallizes.

The ideal crystalline candy is made up of many small crystals that are too small to be felt on the tongue. Instead, they give a creamy feeling to the taste. If the crystals are allowed to become large, the candy would be grainy and undesirable. The size of the crystals depends on the ingredients, the amount of cooking, and the conditions of beating after cooking.

Kinds: There are several basic kinds of candies included in the crystalline category. Fondant is probably the simplest. Although fudge is similar to fondant in its basic ingredients, it also has added ingredients that interfere with crystallization. Penuche is another name for brown sugar fudge and is very similar to the standard fudge. Divinity is also a crystalline candy, but since egg whites are used, it's different from the other types.

How to prepare: Many of the preparations for fondant are basic to the other crystalline candies.

Fondant is versatile and is used as the basis for bonbons and the centers of dipped chocolates. It can be made from just sugar and water, but turns out better if corn syrup or cream of tartar is added. Fondant made with cream of tartar seems to produce a whiter and less sweet fondant with a creamy texture. Both corn syrup and cream of tartar keep crystals small.

During cooking, remove crystals which may form on sides of saucepan. Cover the saucepan during the first few minutes of boiling. After removing the cover, clear away crystals not washed down by the steam with a small brush dipped in water or a damp cloth wrapped around a fork.

When the sugar mixture reaches the proper temperature (soft-ball stage 235°-240°), pour the syrup onto a platter. Do not scrape any of the crystals which may have formed in the pan into the candy mixture. Then allow the candy to cool undisturbed till warm to the touch.

If the fondant is beaten while still hot, only a few large crystals will form and they will grow to a large size, producing grainy candy. But since the syrup is cooled undisturbed, it will form many small crystals simultaneously when it is beaten. And it must be beaten rapidly so that the crystals will separate instead of growing on each other, forming large clusters. For best control, beat the mixture by hand with a wooden spoon.

The syrup will change in appearance throughout this process from a thick, glossy, smooth syrup to a creamy, dull, and lighter-colored mixture.

After cooking and beating are completed, knead fondant to soften and remove any lumps. This produces a creamy candy. Then allow it to ripen in a tightly covered container; usually 12 to 24 hours. Fondant can then be flavored, colored, and chocolate-dipped, if desired.

Sometimes mints are made from a fondantlike mixture that has not been allowed to cool as much.

Small Mints

> 2 cups granulated sugar
> ½ cup light corn syrup
> ⅛ teaspoon cream of tartar
>   Flavored oil
>   Food coloring

In 2-quart saucepan cook sugar, ½ cup water, and corn syrup stirring till sugar dissolves. Cook to thread stage (232°) without stirring. Let stand about 10 minutes.

Add cream of tartar and beat till creamy. Add a few drops of flavored oil and food coloring. Drop mixture from tip of teaspoon onto waxed paper, forming patties. (Keep pan over hot water.) Store mints tightly covered. Makes about 5 dozen mints.

Fudge has a creamy and smooth texture similar to fondant. Unlike many fondants, however, cream or milk is used in the preparation of fudge. Furthermore, chocolate, fat, and corn syrup are often added not only for flavor, but to help produce a candy with small crystals.

Because fudge contains milk and chocolate, it has a tendency to stick to the bottom of the pan and boil over. Stir until the sugar is dissolved and cook it over lower heat. Stir if necessary during cooking.

Add butter after the desired temperature is reached and the flavoring, such as vanilla, during beating. Allow the fudge to cool in the saucepan till bottom of pan feels comfortably warm (110°) before beating. Beat by hand for better control.

You can tell when the fudge has been beaten enough—it stiffens and loses its gloss. Now push the mixture from the saucepan and don't scrape the pan. For neatly shaped pieces, try scoring the fudge while it is still warm.

Coffee Dot Fudge

A mocha-flavored candy—

> 3 cups granulated sugar
> 1 cup milk
> ½ cup light cream
> 2 tablespoons instant coffee powder
> 1 tablespoon light corn syrup
> Dash salt
>
> • • •
>
> 3 tablespoons butter or margarine
> 1 teaspoon vanilla
>
> • • •
>
> ½ 6-ounce package semisweet chocolate pieces (½ cup)
> ½ cup broken pecans
> Pecan halves

Butter sides of heavy 3-quart saucepan. In it combine sugar, milk, cream, instant coffee, corn syrup, and salt. Cook over medium heat, stirring constantly, till sugar dissolves and mixture comes to boiling. Cook to soft-ball stage (234°), stirring only if necessary.

Immediately remove pan from heat; add butter or margarine and cool to lukewarm (110°) without stirring. Add vanilla. Beat vigorously till fudge becomes very thick and starts to lose its gloss. At once stir in semisweet chocolate pieces and broken pecans. Quickly spread in buttered shallow pan or small platter. Score in squares while warm; top each square with a pecan half. Cut when firm.

Creamy, smooth Santa's Fudge, bedecked in colorful Christmas ribbons and ornaments, is perfect for a holiday hostess gift.

Penuche, an old-time favorite, is often called brown sugar fudge because of one of its ingredients. Pecans are traditionally used in this candy. (See *Penuche* for recipe.)

Two-Tone Fudge

A double chocolate candy made with both semi-sweet and milk chocolate—

4½ cups granulated sugar
1 14½-ounce can evaporated milk (1⅔ cups)
½ teaspoon salt

. . .

3 6-ounce packages semisweet chocolate pieces (3 cups)
2 4-ounce milk chocolate candy bars, broken into small pieces

. . .

1 7-ounce jar marshmallow creme
1 cup broken walnuts
1 teaspoon vanilla

In buttered 3-quart saucepan combine sugar, evaporated milk, and salt; bring mixture to boiling. Cook and stir over medium heat to thread stage (230°), about 8 minutes. Remove saucepan from heat.

Working quickly, pour *half* (2 cups) of the mixture over the semisweet chocolate pieces in a bowl, stirring till chocolate is melted. Pat into a buttered 15½x10½x1-inch baking pan.

Add the broken pieces of chocolate candy to the remaining cooked evaporated milk mixture; blend till smooth. Stir in marshmallow creme, broken walnuts, and vanilla. Spread over first layer in baking pan. Chill till firm, at least 1 hour. Makes 5 pounds candy.

Use a candy thermometer for accurate testing of candy "doneness." Clip to side of saucepan after syrup comes to boiling.

Santa's Fudge

2 cups granulated sugar
⅓ cup unsweetened cocoa powder
⅔ cup water
2 tablespoons butter or margarine
1 teaspoon vanilla
½ cup broken walnuts

Butter sides of heavy 3-quart saucepan. In it combine sugar, cocoa, dash salt, water, and butter. Cook over medium heat, stirring constantly, till sugar dissolves and mixture comes to boiling. Cook to soft-ball stage (234°).

Immediately remove pan from heat. Cool to lukewarm (110°) without stirring. Add vanilla. Beat vigorously until fudge becomes very thick and starts to lose its gloss.

Quickly stir in walnuts. Spread in buttered 8x8x2-inch pan. Score in 1-inch squares while warm. Cut fudge into pieces when firm.

Caramel Fudge

2 cups granulated sugar
1 6-ounce can evaporated milk (⅔ cup)
1 10-ounce jar vanilla caramel sauce
2 tablespoons light corn syrup
1 teaspoon vanilla
¼ teaspoon maple flavoring
½ cup chopped walnuts

Butter sides of heavy 2-quart saucepan. In it combine sugar, milk, caramel sauce, and corn syrup. Stir over medium heat till sugar dissolves and mixture comes to boiling. Cook to soft-ball stage (235°), stirring occasionally. Remove from heat. Stir in vanilla and maple flavoring; beat just till mixture begins to lose its gloss. Stir in nuts. Pour into buttered 8x8x2-inch pan. Score into 1½-inch squares while warm; cut fudge into pieces when firm.

To repair fudge that has become too stiff before it is turned into the pan, knead with hands till it softens. Press into buttered pan or shape into a roll, then slice.

For fudge that doesn't set, stir in ¼ cup milk and recook to given temperature. Then beat till correct consistency.

Penuche resembles fudge except the chocolate is omitted and brown sugar is used in addition to granulated sugar. The preparation techniques are similar.

Coconut Penuche

1½ cups granulated sugar
1½ cups brown sugar
1⅓ cups milk
½ teaspoon salt
¼ cup butter or margarine
⅔ cup flaked coconut
2 teaspoons vanilla

In 3-quart saucepan combine sugars, milk, and salt. Cook, stirring constantly, till sugar dissolves and mixture boils. Continue cooking to soft-ball stage (236°), stirring frequently after mixture begins to thicken. Remove from heat. Stir in butter or margarine.

Cool to lukewarm without stirring. Add coconut and vanilla. Beat till mixture loses its gloss and thickens. Turn at once into buttered 8x8x2-inch pan. Cut into squares.

Divinity is a very delicate crystalline candy. Cook the syrup mixture to the hard-ball stage. This very hot syrup cooks the stiffly beaten egg whites as it is slowly added. Beat the mixture constantly while adding syrup. Continue beating till mixture holds its shape. A test can be made by dropping a few spoonfuls onto waxed paper. If it holds its shape, the mixture is ready to add coloring, flavorings, candied fruit, or nuts. Or, the candy can be made with no additional ingredients. The remaining candy is then quickly dropped by teaspoons onto waxed paper.

Cherry Divinity

2½ cups granulated sugar
½ cup light corn syrup
½ cup water
¼ teaspoon salt
• • •
2 egg whites
1 teaspoon vanilla
¼ cup chopped red candied cherries

In 2-quart saucepan combine sugar, corn syrup, water, and salt. Cook to hard-ball stage (260°) stirring only till sugar dissolves. Meanwhile, beat egg whites to stiff peaks. Gradually pour hot syrup over egg whites, beating at high speed on electric mixer. Add vanilla; beat till candy holds its shape, 4 to 5 minutes. Stir in cherries. Quickly drop from teaspoon onto waxed paper. Makes about 40 pieces.

Noncrystalline candy

Candies that are distinguished by their smoothness, indicating absence of crystals, are noncrystalline candies. The syrup is cooked to a very thick, concentrated solution. Then, in order to cool rapidly, it is poured out into a thin layer. This allows the quick formation of a thick, almost solid mass before any crystallization can take place. Ingredients vary with the type of candy being made.

Kinds: There are several main kinds of candies included in the noncrystalline category. Hard candies include brittles as well as the clear, flavored candies which are used for such things as lollipops. Chewy noncrystalline candies include caramels, marshmallows, and taffy.

How to prepare: Cook hard candies to a very high temperature (300° to 310°). It is at this point that the sugar breaks down. This, in addition to the corn syrup that is usually included in the recipe, helps to prevent crystallization. Hard candies are best if made in dry weather. The chewy candies usually have many ingredients that help interfere with crystallization, such as milk, cream, butter, gelatin, chocolate, egg whites, and pectin, in addition to corn syrup.

Brittles and *toffees* are made rich with the addition of butter and they often contain nuts. You can pour these candies onto a greased surface without beating. After the candy is cold, crack it into smaller pieces. If you like, cover the toffees with melted chocolate, then sprinkle with nuts. Toast the nuts for added flavor. Peanut brittle is probably one of the most familiar brittles, but almonds and coconut also add delightful flavors.

Orange-Coconut Brittle

2¼ cups granulated sugar
¼ cup light corn syrup
1 teaspoon shredded orange peel
½ cup orange juice

• • •

2 tablespoons butter or margarine
1 3½-ounce can flaked
   coconut (1⅓ cups)

Butter sides of heavy 3-quart saucepan. In it combine sugar, corn syrup, peel, and orange juice. Cook over medium heat to hard-crack stage (300°), stirring occasionally. Remove from heat; stir in butter. Pour in thin layer into buttered 15½x10½x1-inch pan or large platter. Sprinkle coconut over it evenly. When cold, crack. Makes about 1¼ pounds brittle.

Quick Almond Brittle

An electric skillet makes this treat a quickie—

3 cups granulated sugar
½ cup butter or margarine
   Dash salt
½ cup coarsely chopped almonds
1 6-ounce package semisweet
   chocolate pieces (1 cup)
½ cup finely chopped almonds

Place sugar, butter or margarine, and salt in electric skillet; set temperature at 400°. When sugar begins to melt, stir to blend. Cook and stir till sugar dissolves and color is a light golden brown, about 5 minutes.

Turn control to "off;" stir in coarsely chopped almonds. Pour into buttered 15½x 10½x1-inch pan. Cool. Melt chocolate over very low heat, stirring constantly. Spread over hardened candy. Sprinkle with finely chopped almonds. Break into pieces when cool. Makes about 2 pounds brittle.

Plain hard candies are often colored and flavored with acid or fruit flavors. These candies, if exposed to damp weather, may become sticky, so, keep in tight containers when storing.

The syrup can also be poured over popped corn and nuts for a delicious treat.

Lollipop Clowns

The kids will love these—

3 cups granulated sugar
¾ cup light corn syrup
⅓ cup boiling water
3 tablespoons vinegar
¼ cup butter or margarine
   Dash salt

• • •

Wooden skewers
Fruit-flavored hard-candy circles

In saucepan combine sugar, corn syrup, water, and vinegar; stir till sugar dissolves. Cook to hard-crack stage (300°). Remove from heat. Add butter and salt. Cool until mixture thickens slightly. Quickly drop from tablespoon over wooden skewers placed 5 inches apart on greased cookie sheet to form 3-inch lollipops. Make clown faces with the hard-candy circles. Makes about 16 pops.

Caramel Crunch

1⅓ cups granulated sugar
1 cup butter or margarine
½ cup light corn syrup
1 teaspoon vanilla

• • •

8 cups popped corn
1 cup pecan halves, toasted
1 cup whole almonds, toasted

In 1½-quart saucepan combine sugar, butter, and corn syrup. Bring to boiling over medium heat, stirring constantly. Cook, stirring occasionally, till mixture turns caramel color (soft-crack stage, 290°). Remove from heat and stir in the vanilla.

Pour syrup over popped corn and nuts on buttered shallow baking pan. Separate into clusters with two forks. Store in tightly covered container. Makes about 2 pounds candy.

Brittle—tropical style

Pour hot syrup for Orange-Coconut Brittle → onto a buttered pan or marble slab and let it cool to a crunchy, brittle candy.

Crystal-Cut Candies

    2 cups granulated sugar
    ½ cup light corn syrup
    ½ cup water
       Few drops red *or* green food
          coloring
    4 to 6 drops oil of cinnamon *or*
          oil of wintergreen

In saucepan combine sugar, corn syrup, water, and dash salt. Bring to boiling. Cook to soft-crack stage (290°). Add few drops food coloring and the flavoring; gently swirl mixture to blend. (Use red coloring with cinnamon, green coloring with wintergreen.) Pour into 8x8x2-inch metal pan. Let stand a few minutes till film forms over top of candy.

Mark candy in little puffs, each about ¾-inch square. Because candy is cooler at edges, start marking from outside and work toward the center. Using a broad spatula or pancake turner, press a line across pan ¾ inch from edge, *being careful not to break through the film on surface.* Repeat around other three sides of pan, intersecting lines at corners to form squares. (If lines do not hold shape, candy is not cool enough.) Continue marking lines in candy until center is reached.

While waiting for center to cool enough, retrace previous lines, pressing the spatula deeper *but not breaking film.* When spatula may be pressed to bottom of pan in all lines, candy will be shaped in square puffs. Cool, then turn out and break into pieces. Makes 100 pieces.

Caramels are one of the chewy candies that need no beating after cooking. They usually contain a large amount of corn syrup, or other syrup, and a large amount of cream or milk. The flavor and color of caramels is a result of the reaction between milk and sugar. But the flavor can be varied by adding other ingredients such as coffee, chocolate, or raisins.

Raisin Praline Caramels

    1 cup raisins
    ¾ cup butter or margarine
    1 cup brown sugar
    ½ cup semisweet chocolate pieces

Place raisins in buttered 8x8x2-inch pan. In a saucepan combine butter or margarine and brown sugar. Cook and stir to hard-ball stage (254°). Pour over raisins in pan. Top with semisweet chocolate pieces, spreading as they melt. Chill till firm. Cut in pieces.

Coffee Caramels

    1½ cups light cream
    1 cup granulated sugar
    ½ cup brown sugar
    ½ cup light corn syrup
    ¼ cup butter or margarine
    2 tablespoons instant coffee powder
    1 teaspoon vanilla

In 2-quart saucepan combine cream, granulated sugar, brown sugar, corn syrup, butter, and coffee powder. Cook, stirring constantly, over low heat till sugars dissolve. Cook over medium heat, stirring occasionally, to firm-ball stage (248°). Remove pan from heat. Stir in vanilla. Turn into a 9x5x3-inch pan that has been lined with foil and buttered lightly. Cool. Cut into 3 dozen pieces.

Easy Caramels

For variation, add two squares unsweetened chocolate just after condensed milk—

    1 cup butter or margarine
    1 16-ounce package brown sugar
       (2¼ cups)
       Dash salt
    1 cup light corn syrup
    1 15-ounce can sweetened
       condensed milk (1⅓ cups)
    1 teaspoon vanilla

In a heavy 3-quart saucepan melt butter. Add brown sugar and salt, stirring till thoroughly combined. Blend in corn syrup. Gradually add sweetened condensed milk, stirring constantly. Cook and stir over medium heat to firm-ball stage (245°), 12 to 15 minutes. Remove from heat and stir in vanilla.

Pour into buttered 9x9x2-inch pan. Cool thoroughly. Cut in small squares. Enclose each piece in clear plastic wrap, if desired. Makes about 2½ pounds candy.

Taffy is not quite as rich as caramels. After pouring the syrup mixture onto an oiled surface, allow it to cool just enough so that it can be handled. Then pull it until light in color, porous, and hard to pull. Coat fingers with butter to keep candy from sticking as it is being pulled. When the taffy is ready, pull it into a long rope and with a buttered scissors, quickly snip into bite-size pieces. Wrap each separately in waxed paper; twist ends of wrapper.

Marshmallows are a soft candy made with gelatin and sometimes egg white. They have a proportionately large amount of corn syrup. Cook the sugar syrup to a temperature about the same as for divinity, then add softened gelatin and beat the mixture till fluffy. An electric mixer is almost a must for this candy.

Shortcut candy

A third group of candy that is an assortment of different types are the shortcut candies. Most are not cooked to any specified temperature, but usually are cooked for a definite time.

Other candies included in this group are the uncooked type. These include the candies made with confectioners' sugar and ingredients such as melted butter, melted chocolate, concentrated milk products or other liquid, and foods that are added for flavor.

Since all of these candies are easier to prepare, the beginning candy maker may have more success with them. They can range from tiny mints made from a frosting mix to cereal and nut favorites.

Chocolate Peanut Pillows

In saucepan melt one 6-ounce package semisweet chocolate pieces (1 cup) and 1 tablespoon shortening over low heat. Remove from heat and stir in ½ cup peanut butter and 2 tablespoons confectioners' sugar.

Using two forks, dip 3 cups spoon-size shredded wheat biscuits into chocolate mixture, coating all sides. Gently shake off excess chocolate. Roll pieces in ½ cup finely chopped peanuts. Cool on rack. Store in refrigerator or in a very cool place. Makes about 3 cups.

Peanut Clusters

    1 3¾- or 4-ounce package *regular* chocolate pudding mix
    1 cup granulated sugar
    ½ cup evaporated milk
    1 tablespoon butter or margarine
        . . .
    1 cup salted peanuts
    1 teaspoon vanilla

In heavy saucepan combine pudding mix, sugar, milk, and butter. Cook and stir over medium heat till mixture boils. Reduce heat; cook and stir 3 minutes longer. Remove from heat; quickly stir in nuts and vanilla. Beat by hand till candy thickens and begins to lose its gloss. Drop from teaspoon into clusters on waxed paper. Makes 24 pieces.

Caramel Chocolate Clusters

Rice cereal can be substituted for noodles—

In a small saucepan combine 15 vanilla caramels (4 ounces), ¼ cup semisweet chocolate pieces, 2 tablespoons chunk-style peanut butter, and 2 tablespoons water. Cook and stir over low heat till caramels are completely melted and mixture is well combined.

Pour over 2 cups chow mein noodles; stir gently till noodles are evenly coated with caramel mixture. Drop from teaspoon onto waxed paper. Let stand till firm. Makes 30 pieces.

Angel Sweets

    1 6-ounce package semisweet chocolate pieces (1 cup)
    2 tablespoons butter or margarine
    1 egg
        . . .
    1 cup sifted confectioners' sugar
    1 cup chopped walnuts
    2 cups miniature marshmallows
    ½ cup flaked coconut

In saucepan melt chocolate and butter over low heat. Remove from heat; blend in egg. Stir in sugar, nuts, and marshmallows, blending well. Shape into 1-inch balls; roll in coconut. Chill. Makes about 48 pieces.

Confection Bars

½ cup butter or margarine
¼ cup granulated sugar
⅓ cup unsweetened cocoa powder
1 teaspoon vanilla
1 slightly beaten egg
1 3½-ounce can flaked coconut
    (1⅓ cups)
2 cups vanilla wafer crumbs

. . .

3 tablespoons milk
2 tablespoons *regular* vanilla
    pudding mix
½ cup butter or margarine
2 cups sifted confectioners'
    sugar
1 4-ounce bar sweet cooking
    chocolate
1 tablespoon butter or margarine

Combine ½ cup butter, ¼ cup sugar, cocoa powder, and vanilla in top of double boiler; cook and stir over hot water till blended. Add egg; cook 5 minutes. Stir in coconut and vanilla wafer crumbs. Press into 9x9x2-inch pan; let stand 15 minutes.

Combine milk and dry pudding mix. Cream the ½ cup butter and confectioners' sugar. Add the pudding mixture and beat till smooth. Spread over first layer. Chill about 15 minutes or till firm. Melt sweet chocolate with the 1 tablespoon butter; cool and spread on second layer. Cut in squares. Makes 3 dozen bars.

Mint Swirls

3 tablespoons butter or margarine
3 tablespoons milk
1 package creamy white frosting
    mix (for 2-layer cake)
8 drops oil of peppermint
    Few drops red food coloring

Melt butter with milk in top of double boiler. Add frosting mix; stir till smooth. Cook over rapidly boiling water for 5 minutes, stirring occasionally. Add oil of peppermint. Tint with food coloring. Drop by teaspoon onto waxed paper, swirling tops of candies with teaspoon. (Keep candy over hot water while dropping candies. If mixture thickens, add a few drops hot water.) Cool. Makes about 60 mints.

Caramel Snappers

144 small pecan halves (about
    1 cup)
36 vanilla caramels
½ cup semisweet chocolate
    pieces, melted

Grease cookie sheet. On it arrange pecans, flat side down, in groups of 4. Place 1 caramel on each cluster of pecans. Heat at 325° till caramels soften, about 4 to 8 minutes. (Watch carefully, various caramels melt at different rates.)

Remove from the oven; with buttered spatula, flatten caramel over pecans. Cool slightly; remove from pan to waxed paper. Swirl melted chocolate on top. Makes 36 pieces.

Dewdrops

In heavy 2-quart saucepan combine one 3- or 3¼-ounce package *regular* vanilla pudding mix, 1 cup granulated sugar, and one 6-ounce can evaporated milk (⅔ cup). Cook and stir over medium-high heat till mixture comes to boiling. Cook at a *full rolling boil* 5 minutes, stirring constantly. Remove from heat.

Add 1 tablespoon butter or margarine and 1 teaspoon vanilla. Turn into small mixer bowl and beat with electric mixer at high speed for 3 to 4 minutes, or till mixture holds its shape.

Stir in ½ cup chopped walnuts and ¼ cup chopped red candied cherries. Drop from rounded teaspoons onto waxed paper or buttered baking sheet. Top with candied cherry halves, if desired. Makes about 24 pieces.

Chocolate-coated candy

By chocolate coating a variety of candies you can turn them into delectable treats. Dip caramels, nuts, candied fruit, toffee, nougats, or molded fondant. (Mold fondant centers a day before dipping so fondant won't leak through the chocolate.)

For best results, don't attempt chocolate dipping on a hot or damp day. A dry, cool day and a room temperature around 65° are the ideal working conditions.

Use at least 1 pound grated semisweet candy-making chocolate. Place in top of double boiler over hot water (115° to 120°) with the water touching the pan holding the chocolate. Stir until chocolate melts. Exchange hot water for cold water in bottom of double boiler. Stir and cool chocolate to 83°. Exchange the cold water for warm water (85°).

Working quickly, drop center into chocolate and roll to coat centers. Remove with a fork. Draw fork across rim of pan to remove excess chocolate. Place on a wire rack over waxed paper, bringing "string" of chocolate across the top of each. If chocolate becomes too stiff, heat as at first; continue dipping.

Chocolate-coated candy takes lots of experience and patience along with practice to be able to produce candy that looks like the professionally dipped candies.

CANE SUGAR—The sugar produced from the sugar cane plant. Over half the sugar used for cooking and eating is cane sugar with the remainder being made from sugar beets. (See *Sugar, Sugar Cane* for additional information.)

CANETON (*kan tôn'*)—The French term for duckling. *Caneton à l'Orange,* a popular French dish, is duckling served with an orange and lemon sauce. (See also *Duck.*)

CANNELLONI (*kan' uh lō' nē*) — Italian stuffed noodle rolls served as an hors d'oeuvre or entrée. They are stuffed, then baked in a sauce and sprinkled with cheese. (See also *Italian Cookery.*)

Shortcut candies include Dewdrops, made from a pudding mix, and Caramel Snappers, using purchased caramels. Let the kids help make Caramel Snappers since they're so simply made.

CANNING

*How to preserve fruits, vegetables, and meats
with instructions for each canning method.*

Canning is a preservation method by which food is sealed in containers and is usually processed with heat. During the processing time, heat cooks the food and renders it safe for shelf storage at room temperature.

The principles of canning were first established by a Frenchman named Nicolas Appert. In 1809, he was awarded a prize by Napoleon for developing a food preservation method that eased the problem of providing food for the French Army. Appert's method involved heating food in sealed containers. At the time, Appert did not understand the true reason for food preservation. He believed the food did not spoil because it was sealed in an airtight container, when in fact it was the destruction of bacteria by heat that was responsible. This was explained by Louis Pasteur more than a half-century later.

In 1819, ten years after Appert chanced on his method for canning food, the development of commercial canning began in America. The development of home canning methods is credited to the more adventurous homemakers with their successful, yet crude efforts to preserve the excess food produced during the bountiful harvests. Later came the advanced home canning methods in use today.

The success of canning is dependent upon the destruction of microorganisms and/or enzymes which may cause spoilage. Commercially canned food which is heated to destroy these agents is termed commercially sterile. However, it is not possible always to destroy all microorganisms that are present. A few heat-resistant organisms can only be destroyed by heating to such high temperatures that the food in turn becomes undesirable. Fortunately, these types of organisms need not be destroyed since they are harmless.

Obviously the selection of high-quality food is of the utmost importance. Regardless of whether food is canned commercially or at home, the chance for spoilage is greater in food which has started to decay than in food which is of top quality.

Nutritional value: Canning does not significantly change the nutrient value of food. There is little difference in raw or canned food in caloric, protein, fat, or carbohydrate content. However, a slight-to-moderate loss of some of the less-stable vitamins does occur during processing, and other vitamins and minerals dissolve out of the food and into the liquid surrounding the food. This can be remedied easily by serving the canning liquid with the food. This liquid is often termed "the elixir of life."

How to store: Both commercially canned and home canned food are safe for shelf storage although a loss of quality may be noted over a prolonged period of time. If food is canned at home, always label the container with (1) date of canning, and (2) kind of food. By knowing this information, the food can be used accordingly to avoid excessively long periods of storage.

Regardless of whether food is canned commercially or at home, it is best stored in a dry place at a moderately cool temperature. Avoid storage near hot water pipes, radiators, or kitchen ranges. If glass jars are used, storage in the dark may help

Preserving the bountiful harvest

Garden-fresh vegetables remain in season → throughout the year just as jellies and jams prolong the fruit season when canned.

preserve the natural color of the food. Unless the seal of the container is broken, canned food will not spoil when frozen. However, a softening of texture usually results, making the food less desirable.

Some commercially canned foods, such as the larger canned hams, require special storage. These hams have been pasteurized but have not been canned by conventional methods. They should be refrigerated before opening. However, some of the smaller hams canned by conventional methods are shelf stable. It is necessary always to check the label on the container for special storage instructions.

After commercially canned *or* home canned food is opened, it should be refrigerated. Any unused portion of food may be stored safely in the open can, provided it is covered and placed in the refrigerator.

How to use: Home canned meats, poultry, fish, and vegetables (except tomatoes) must be heated at boiling temperature for 10 to 20 minutes before tasting or using. This is important since some forms of spoilage are not visible. By boiling, you will destroy any unknown spoilage agents.

Due to the more scientifically controlled conditions under which foods are canned commercially, they need not undergo the same precautionary period of cooking required for home canned foods. Commercially canned foods, unless labeled otherwise, can be eaten directly from the can without heating. The same is true of home canned fruits and tomatoes.

Commercial canning

Scientific advances in microbiology in addition to the development and refinement of equipment paved the way for the growth of the canning industry. As a result, food canned by commercial methods has met wide acceptance since it offers a convenient and safe means for preserving food.

Canned food is more easily transported than many fresh foods and does not require refrigeration necessary for fresh or frozen foods. Likewise, the storage of canned food in the home is often less costly than the storage of fresh or frozen food. Also, canning makes many seasonal foods available the year round. Thus, canned food often provides the homemaker with a wider selection of food at a lower cost.

Equipment: At first the containers used for canning were wide-mouthed glass bottles sealed with corks. Later experimentation with earthenware containers proved unsuccessful. In time, however, the more efficient and economic tin containers were accepted in the canning industry. The earliest tin cans were filled through small openings in the top. Later, open-topped containers, which could be sealed after filling, were developed for commercial use.

Today, containers made of steel plate coated with tin are used. Some foods, such as red fruits and certain vegetables, may discolor if they are canned in tin. Consequently, containers used in canning these foods are coated with a special enamel finish. In addition, glass containers with tight seals are sometimes used by commercial canners for canning food.

Methods of canning: The conventional method of commercial canning is similar to home canning methods. After the food is sealed in the container, it is heated (usually under pressure) for a certain length of time, depending upon the type of food. Then after processing, the containers are cooled quickly to stop the cooking.

While heating the food destroys bacteria, it does present certain problems to the canner. For example, since heat must travel from the outside of the container to the center, there is a tendency to overcook food near the edge of the container. To overcome this, new methods and equipment are continually being developed.

In one method, cans are agitated during processing in an attempt to speed up the distribution of heat throughout the food. Likewise, higher temperatures and shorter processing times are utilized.

Another method employs even higher temperatures and shorter processing times. After the food is sterilized, it is packed into sterilized containers under aseptic conditions. A variation of this method involves packing sterilized food into sterilized containers under pressure. A short processing is sometimes used after sealing.

Common container sizes

Check labels for exact net weights as different foods packed in identical containers vary in weight due to different densities.

Container size	Approximate net weight or fluid measure	Approximate Cups
8 ounce	8 ounces	1
Picnic	10½ to 12 ounces	1¼
12 ounce (vacuum)	12 ounces	1½
No. 300	14 to 16 ounces	1¾
No. 303	16 to 17 ounces	2
No. 2	20 ounces or 18 fluid ounces	2½
No. 2½	27 to 29 ounces	3½
No. 3 cylinder or 46 fluid ounce	51 ounces or 46 fluid ounces	5¾
No. 10	6½ pounds to 7 pounds 5 ounces	12 to 13

How to select: When purchasing canned food, avoid cans which bulge or cans in which there is evidence that the seal has been broken. A dented or rusted can is safe so long as the seal has not been broken.

Be certain to read carefully the label on the can. It not only states the brand name, but also the name of the food, the name of the manufacturer or distributor, and the net weight or volume of the contents. There may be an illustration, a description of the contents in terms of variety, the style of pack (water or syrup—light, heavy, or extra heavy), the amount of food in the can stated in cups or number of pieces, or suggested serving ideas and recipes.

The concern for special diets has not gone unnoticed by the canning industry.

Today, a wide selection of special dietetic foods, canned without the addition of salt, sugar, or with less fat, is available in the supermarket and specialty stores.

Home canning

Foods canned at home are popular with many families not only for economy, but also for a "fresh-from-your-garden" flavor possible for home canned fruits and vegetables. In addition to these foods, meats, poultry, jams, jellies, relishes, and pickles are often canned at home.

The three methods of canning recommended for home canning of food are (1) raw pack, (2) hot pack, and (3) open kettle. Food prepared by either the raw or hot pack method is then processed in a (1) pressure canner, (2) pressure saucepan, or (3) water bath canner. Food canned by the open kettle method is not processed since the food is thoroughly cooked before it is placed in the containers. A specific canning and processing method is often recommended for canning a particular food. (For best results, follow the canning and processing methods outlined below and in the accompanying charts.)

Equipment: Although you may purchase some equipment made especially for canning, many items may already be available in your kitchen. For example, brushes, knives, colanders, sieves, and scales are useful in canning. A large wire basket or similar utensil is convenient for blanching (dipping food into boiling water) fruits and vegetables. A funnel or ladle is handy for filling containers. In addition, large tongs are necessary for handling hot jars or cans after the processing.

For water bath canning, you need a big, tightly covered metal container. It should be deep enough for an inch or two of water over the tops of the jars plus a few inches for brisk boiling. A large rack placed in the bottom of the canner can be used for holding the jars. This prevents direct contact between the containers and the canner, and if the rack has handles, provides easy removal of hot jars.

A pressure canner is required for canning food under pressure. Check the pressure gauge for accuracy and never attempt to use a pressure canner which is not working properly. If you process only a small amount of food and use small containers, a pressure saucepan may be substituted.

The selection of containers for canning is important. Use either glass jars, or cans made of steel plate coated with tin. Personal preference as well as the particular food to be canned will determine the final selection of containers that are used.

There are many advantages to using glass jars in home canning: although the initial expense of glass is greater than for cans, jars can be used and reused for many years; the sealing lid or rubber is the only part that must be replaced with each canning; less equipment is required for sealing glass jars than is needed for metal containers, and many homemakers prefer to use jars because the food can be seen after canning. The pride of many home canning enthusiasts is the attractive pack visible only in glass containers. Another advantage to choosing glass containers is that they may be used for canning all foods. This is particularly important when canning red fruits, pumpkin, rhubarb, winter squash, corn, and hominy as they may become discolored unless glass or enamel-coated metal containers are used.

But this is not to suggest metal cans do not have some advantages: cans, if not dented or damaged, can be used for more than one canning; since the sealing is done by a mechanical sealer before processing, there is no loss of liquid from cans regardless of fluctuation in pressure; a more rapid cooling after processing is possible with metal, and metal cans protect food from light thus preventing discoloration of the food during storage. These are distinct advantages over glass jar canning where the sealing does not occur until after processing, and where a rapid loss of pressure may cause loss of liquid or even breakage of the container during canning.

Different-sized containers—glass or metal—are available and should be selected according to the amount of food to be canned, the storage available, the size of family, and intended use of the food.

The two most common types of covers for glass jars are (1) a metal lid edged with a sealing compound which is secured to the jar with a metal screw band, and (2) a zinc porcelain-lined cover with a shoulder rubber ring. Either of these covers works satisfactorily; however, they should be checked before each use. Brittle or inelastic rubber rings and new metal sealing discs must be replaced before each canning. Since sealing compounds differ, always follow the lid manufacturer's directions for the correct method of use.

The sealing of metal cans is accomplished with a continuous ring of sealing compound which is found around the edge of the lid. When heated, the sealing compound melts and seals the container.

Methods of canning: The preliminary steps to canning involve preparing and packing the food into the containers. Three methods—raw pack, hot pack, and open kettle—may be used. However, each method is recommended only for certain foods. These recommendations are based upon safety and quality retention of the food.

Raw pack method—the uncooked food is packed into the containers and then a boiling liquid—syrup, water, or fruit juice— is added. Processing can be done either in a water bath or in a pressure cooker. The raw pack method is recommended for canning most fruits and tomatoes. Other vegetables may be canned raw pack *if they are processed in a pressure canner.*

Hot pack method—the food is partially cooked before it is packed into the containers. This method is used in canning vegetables, meats, and some fruits. Although most fruits may be canned either raw or hot pack, apples, applesauce, and rhubarb are recommended for hot pack.

Open kettle canning—the food is cooked (but not necessarily sterilized) before it is sealed in the containers and no further processing is required. This method of canning is recommended for jams, jellies, preserves, conserves, fruit butters, and other foods relatively high in sugar or acid.

Methods of processing: Processing is the correct application of heat to food packed in containers to render it safe for storage: over processing results in overcooked food that is still safe for storage, underprocessed food is unsafe. Processing can be done in a pressure canner or cooker, pressure saucepan, or water bath canner.

Pressure canner or cooker—this is necessary for low-acid foods such as meats and vegetables (except tomatoes, sauerkraut, and ripe pimiento peppers), since in low-acid foods some spoilage agents are not destroyed by boiling temperatures, and therefore, higher temperatures are necessary. This is possible only when a pressure canner or cooker is used.

To use a pressure canner, stand the containers on a rack in the bottom of the canner in two to three inches of water, leaving a small space between each container. Fasten the cover securely and allow the steam to escape steadily for ten minutes before closing the pet cock or vent.

The processing time begins when the pressure gauge reaches a specified pressure. Maintain the pressure at a constant point by adjusting the heat under the canner. Do not attempt to lower the pressure by opening the pet cock or vent as this will cause a loss of liquid from the jars. When the processing time is up, first remove the canner from the heat, then let the pressure drop gradually to zero before opening the pet cock or vent. Then open the cover and carefully remove the containers with tongs. Cool containers on a rack or cloth, a few inches apart, and away from drafts.

Altitude correction

For water bath canning, add 1 minute to processing time if time specified is 20 minutes or less, for each 1,000 feet above sea level. Add 2 minutes for every 1,000 feet if time called for is more than 20 minutes.

For pressure canning, increase pressure 1 pound for each 2,000 feet above sea level.

Pressure saucepan—this can be used for processing pints or other small containers. It must be equipped with a gauge for showing and maintaining a constant pressure of ten pounds. For processing times, add 20 minutes to the time recommended for processing in a pressure canner. Follow the manufacturer's instructions for detailed canning directions.

Water bath canner—this is used for processing high-acid foods such as fruits, tomatoes, sauerkraut, ripe pimiento peppers, and pickles. Place the containers in a large kettle and fill to one inch above the tops of the containers with water that is just below the boiling point. Arrange the containers so they are not touching, then cover the kettle. The processing time begins when the water comes to a full boil. Keep the water boiling gently. If necessary, add more boiling water to keep tops of containers covered. When time is up, remove the containers and place them on a rack or cloth, positioned a few inches apart, and away from all drafts.

Home canned fruits

Select fresh, firm fruits for canning. To insure even cooking, sort fruit according to size and ripeness. Thoroughly wash fruit under running water or through several changes of water; handle fruit gently to avoid bruising. Use ascorbic acid color keeper on apples, peaches, and pears to prevent the cut surfaces of the fruit from darkening during preparation. Most fruits may be canned either raw pack or hot pack. However, they are most often processed in a water bath canner. To can fruits, follow detailed directions below.

1. Check jars and lids for flaws. Discard any with chips or cracks. Use all new metal sealing discs or rubbers.

2. Wash jars in hot, sudsy water; rinse. Wash lids according to manufacturer's directions. Place jars in hot water till ready to use. They needn't be sterilized as this is done during the processing.

3. Place water bath canner on heat with enough water to cover tops of jars.

4. Prepare fruit according to chart (see page 395) using either the raw or hot pack method. Use a thin, medium, or heavy syrup to suit personal taste.

Raw pack: (May be used for all fruits except apples, applesauce, and rhubarb.) Firmly pack fruit into jars. Leave ½-inch headspace at top of jar. Pour in boiling syrup, still leaving ½-inch headspace.

Hot pack: (May be used for all fruits.) Precook fruit in syrup according to chart. Loosely pack hot fruit into jars leaving ½-inch headspace (¼-inch headspace for applesauce). Cover fruit with boiling syrup, leaving the same amount of headspace.

5. Force out air bubbles from filled jars by working blade of table knife down sides of jars. Add more liquid if needed, but keep the original headspace.

6. Adjust jar caps: (a) For *two-piece metal lids,* wipe sealing edge of jar with clean cloth to remove food particles; put metal lid on jar with sealing compound next to glass. Screw band tight. (b) For *porcelain-lined zinc screw covers,* fit wet rubber ring on jar; wipe jar rim and ring with clean cloth. Partially seal by screwing the zinc cover down firmly, then turn the cover back ¼ inch.

7. Lower jars on rack into the water bath canner (have water just below the boiling point). Be sure jars do not touch. Cover the canner. The processing time begins when the water returns to a rolling boil. Boil gently during entire processing time. Add more *boiling* water as needed to keep jars covered. Process fruit according to the time indicated on chart. Note altitude corrections (see page 393).

8. After processing, remove hot jars from canner. Cool on rack or cloth, a few inches apart, and away from drafts for time specified by lid manufacturer.

To release air bubbles, work blade of table knife down side of filled jar. This insures all food is covered with liquid.

9. Check seals on jars when cold. To test jar with metal lid, press center of lid; if lid is drawn down, jar is sealed. For other types of covers, tip jar to check for leakage. If jar isn't sealed, use immediately; or, check jar for flaws and reprocess with a new lid following original procedure.

10. To store jars, remove screw bands from two-piece metal lids. Wipe jars; label with contents and date. Store in cool, dry, and dark place for up to one year.

When ready to use canned fruit, puncture metal disc and lift up. For zinc screw covers, pull out rubber ring, using pliers, before unscrewing cap. Look for spoilage —leaks, bulging lids, or off-odor. Never taste food with these signs; discard.

Home canned meats

Meat may be canned using the raw or hot pack method. Do not add liquid to meat if canned raw pack. Meat must be processed in a pressure canner. Follow instructions for canning meat as given below.

1. Check jars and lids for flaws. Discard any with chips or cracks. Use all new metal sealing discs or rubbers.

2. Wash jars in hot, sudsy water; rinse. Wash lids according to manufacturer's directions. Place jars in hot water till ready to use. They needn't be sterilized.

Canned fruit yield

Generally, for 1 quart canned fruit use the following amount of fresh fruit as purchased:

Fruit	Pounds
Apples	2½ to 3
Berries, except strawberries	1½ to 3
Cherries (if canned unpitted)	2 to 2½
Peaches	2 to 3
Pears	2 to 3
Plums	1½ to 2½

Canning fruit			
Fruit	Preparation of Fruit Thin Syrup—2 cups sugar to 4 cups water. Yield 5 cups. Medium Syrup—3 cups sugar to 4 cups water. Yield 5½ cups. Heavy Syrup—4¾ cups sugar to 4 cups water. Yield 6½ cups. (Boil sugar and water together 5 minutes. Skim if needed. Figure ½ to 1½ cups sugar for each quart jar.)	Water bath in minutes (Pints)	Water bath in minutes (Quarts)
Apples	*Hot Pack:* Wash, pare, core, and cut in pieces. While preparing, treat to prevent darkening with ascorbic acid color keeper following package directions for fresh-cut fruit. Boil in syrup or water 5 minutes. Pack hot; cover with boiling syrup or water leaving ½-inch headspace. Adjust lids; process in boiling water bath.	15	20
	Applesauce: Prepare sauce; heat to simmering; pack hot into hot jars leaving ¼-inch headspace. Adjust lids; process in boiling water bath.	10	10
Apricots Peaches Pears	*Raw Pack:* Wash and peel fruit (dip peaches and apricots in boiling water, then in cold water for easier peeling) *or* omit peeling apricots, if desired. Halve or slice; pit or core. While preparing, use ascorbic acid color keeper following package directions for fresh-cut fruit. Pack into hot jars; cover with boiling syrup leaving ½-inch headspace. Adjust lids; process in boiling water bath.	25	30
	Hot Pack: Prepare as above. Heat through in syrup. Pack hot into hot jars; cover with boiling syrup leaving ½-inch headspace. Adjust lids; process in boiling water bath.	20	25
Berries (except strawberries)	*Raw Pack:* Use for raspberries, other soft berries. Wash fruit; drain. Fill hot jars. Cover with boiling syrup leaving ½-inch headspace. Adjust lids; process in boiling water bath.	10	15
	Hot Pack: Use for firm berries. Wash; drain. Add ½ cup sugar to each quart berries. Bring to boil in covered pan; shake pan to keep berries from sticking. Pack hot into hot jars leaving ½-inch headspace. Adjust lids; process in boiling water bath.	10	15
Cherries	*Raw Pack:* Wash, stem, and pit, if desired. Fill hot jars. Cover with boiling syrup leaving ½-inch headspace. Adjust lids; process in boiling water bath.	20	25
	Hot Pack: Wash; remove pits, if desired. Add ½ cup sugar to each quart fruit. Add a little water only to *unpitted* cherries. Cover; bring to boiling. Pack hot into hot jars leaving ½-inch headspace. Adjust lids; process in boiling water bath.	10	15
Plums	*Raw Pack:* Wash; prick skins if canning whole fruit. Halve and pit freestone plums, if desired. Pack into hot jars. Cover with boiling syrup leaving ½-inch headspace. Adjust lids; process in boiling water bath.	20	25
	Hot Pack: Prepare as above. Bring to boil in syrup. Pack hot into hot jars; add boiling syrup leaving ½-inch headspace. Adjust lids; process in boiling water bath.	20	25
Rhubarb	Wash; cut into ½-inch pieces. Add ½ cup sugar per quart fruit; let stand till juicy. Bring to boil. Pack into hot jars; leave ½-inch headspace. Adjust lids; process in boiling water bath.	10	10
Fruit juices	Wash fruit; pit, if desired. Crush fruit; heat to simmering; strain through cheesecloth bag. Add sugar, if desired (1 cup per gallon of juice). Heat to simmering. Fill hot jars with hot juice leaving ½-inch headspace. Adjust lids; process in boiling water bath.	5	5

3. Clean and prepare meat or poultry according to chart (see below).

4. Pack meat into jars using either the raw or hot pack method.

Raw pack: Loosely pack raw meat in jars, leaving 1-inch headspace. Don't add liquid. Set open jars in large pan with warm water two inches below rim of jars; cover pan. Simmer till temperature is 170° in center of jars, about 75 minutes.

Hot pack: Cook meat or poultry in a small amount of water or broth till medium done. (If desired, remove bones from poultry.) Loosely pack cooked meat into jars, leaving 1-inch headspace. Cover with broth or boiling water, leaving 1-inch headspace. Force out air bubbles from filled jars by working blade of table knife down sides of jars. Add more liquid if needed, but keep original 1-inch headspace.

5. Add 1 teaspoon salt to each quart.

6. Adjust jar caps: (a) For *two-piece metal lids,* wipe jar rim with clean cloth to remove grease or food; put metal lid on jar with sealing compound next to glass. Screw band tight. (b) For *porcelain-lined zinc screw covers,* fit wet rubber ring on jar; wipe jar rim and ring with cloth. Partially seal by screwing zinc cap down firmly, then turn the cover back ¼ inch.

7. Place jars on rack in pressure canner containing two to three inches of hot water. Leave a small amount of space between the jars. Securely fasten cover. Let the steam escape steadily for ten minutes before closing the pet cock or vent. The processing time begins when the gauge reaches a specified pressure. Keep pressure constant. Process according to chart. Note altitude corrections (see page 393).

Canning meat			
Meat	Preparation of Meat Chill meat immediately after slaughter. Pack meat loosely in jars leaving 1-inch headspace at top of jar. Add 1 teaspoon salt per quart, if desired.	Pressure canner minutes at 10 lbs. (Pints)	Pressure canner minutes at 10 lbs. (Quarts)
Beef Veal Lamb Pork Venison	Wipe with clean, damp cloth. Soak venison in salt water (¼ cup salt to 1 quart water) 1 to 2 hours; drain. Cut meat in jar-length pieces so grain runs length of jar; or cube. Remove gristle, bones, and as much fat as possible. *Raw Pack:* Pack raw meat loosely in jars; leave 1-inch headspace. Add no liquid. Set open jars in deep pan with warm water 2 inches below rim of jars; cover. Simmer till temperature reaches 170° in center of jars; or till medium done, about 75 minutes. Add salt. Adjust lids; process in pressure canner. *Hot Pack:* Cook meat, covered, in small amount water till medium done; stir occasionally. Pack jars loosely leaving 1-inch headspace. Add salt. Cover with broth or boiling water leaving 1-inch headspace. Adjust lids; process in pressure canner.	75 75	90 90
Poultry Chicken Duck Turkey Game Birds Rabbit	Rinse poultry thoroughly in cold water. Soak rabbit in salt water (¼ cup salt to 1 quart water) 1 to 2 hours. Wipe; cut up. *Raw Pack:* Remove bone but not skin or leave bone in. Pack loosely into jars. (For poultry, place thigh and drumsticks with skin next to glass and fit breasts into center.) Leave 1-inch headspace. Set open jars in large pan with warm water 2 inches below rim of jars. Cover and simmer till temperature reaches 170° in center of jars or till medium done (almost no pink when cut in center), about 75 minutes. Add salt, if desired; adjust lids; process in pressure canner. *Hot Pack:* Cook poultry covered in small amount hot broth or water till almost no pink shows when cut in center. Remove bones or leave bones in. Pack loosely into jars. (For poultry, place thigh and drumstick with skin next to glass and fit breasts in center.) Leave 1-inch headspace; add salt, if desired. Cover with boiling broth leaving 1-inch headspace. Adjust lids; process in pressure canner.	boned 75 bone-in 65 boned 75 bone-in 65	90 75 90 75

8. When time is up, remove center from heat; let the pressure drop to zero. Then open the pet cock slowly; unfasten the cover. Remove jars. Cool on cloth or rack, a few inches apart, and away from drafts for the time specified by lid manufacturer.

9. Check seal on jars when cold. To test jar with metal lid, press center of lid; if lid is drawn down, the jar is sealed. For other types of caps, tip jar to check for leakage. If jar isn't sealed, use immediately; or, check jar for flaws and reprocess immediately with a new lid.

10. To store jars, remove screw band from two-piece metal lid. Wipe jars; label with contents and date. Store in cool, dry, and dark place for up to one year.

When ready to use canned meat or poultry, puncture metal disc and lift up. For zinc screw covers, pull out rubber ring, using pliers, before unscrewing cap. Look for spoilage—leaks, bulging lids, or off-odor. Never taste foods with these signs. Boil all meat 20 minutes before tasting.

Home canned vegetables

Most vegetables may be canned either raw or hot pack. The method used is a matter of personal preference. However, all vegetables (except tomatoes, sauerkraut, and ripe pimiento peppers) must be processed in a pressure canner for safety. Tomatoes and other high-acid vegetables are generally processed in a water bath canner.

Select fresh, firm vegetables for canning. Sort according to size to insure even cooking if vegetables are canned whole, such as beets, mushrooms, or new potatoes. Also, sort according to ripeness. Follow detailed instructions given below.

1. Check jars and lids for flaws. Discard any with chips or cracks. Use all new metal sealing discs or rubbers.

2. Wash jars in hot, sudsy water; rinse. Wash lids according to manufacturer's directions. Place jars in hot water till ready to use. They needn't be sterilized as this is done during processing

3. Wash and trim vegetables according to chart (see pages 398-399). For tomatoes, follow recipe directions (see page 400).

4. Pack vegetables into jars using either the raw or hot pack method.

Raw pack: Asparagus, lima beans, green beans, carrots, corn, and peas may be packed by this method. (Can cream-style corn in pint jars only.) Firmly pack raw vegetables into hot jars (except pack limas, corn, and peas loosely). Leave ½-inch headspace at top of jar (1 inch for limas, corn, and peas; 1½ inches for cream-style corn). Pour boiling water into jars leaving ½-inch headspace (1½ inches for peas).

Hot pack: All vegetables may be packed by this method. Precook vegetables for time indicated on chart. Loosely pack boiling vegetables into hot jars; leave ½-inch headspace (1 inch for limas, corn, peas, and sweet potatoes). Add boiling liquid; leave same headspace as above.

5. Force out air bubbles from filled jars by working blade of table knife down sides of jars. Add more liquid if needed, but keep the original headspace.

6. Add 1 teaspoon salt to each quart. (If desired, salt may be omitted.)

7. Adjust jar caps: (a) For *two-piece metal lids,* wipe jar rim with clean cloth to remove food particles; put metal lid on jar with sealing compound next to glass. Screw band tight. (b) For *porcelain-lined zinc screw covers,* fit wet rubber ring on jar; wipe jar rim and ring with clean cloth. Partially seal by screwing cap down firmly, then turn cap back ¼ inch.

8. Place jars on rack in pressure canner containing two to three inches hot water. Leave small amount of space between jars. Fasten cover securely. Let a steady flow of steam escape for two minutes before closing pet cock or vent. Processing time begins when the gauge reaches the specified pressure. Keep pressure constant. Process according to chart. Note altitude corrections (see page 393).

9. When time is up, remove canner from heat; let pressure drop to zero. Open pet cock or vent slowly; unfasten cover. Remove jars with tongs. Cool on rack or cloth, a few inches apart, and away from drafts for time specified by lid manufacturer.

10. Check seal on jars when cold. To test metal lid, press center of lid; if lid is drawn down, jar is sealed. For other caps, tip jars to check for leakage. If not sealed, use immediately; or, check for flaws and reprocess immediately with a new lid.

Canning vegetables			
Vegetable	Preparation of Vegetables Precook; pack into jar with hot cooking water to ½ inch from top unless otherwise specified; add 1 teaspoon salt to each quart. Or pack raw; cover with boiling water. Leave ½-inch headspace (1½ inches for peas); add 1 teaspoon salt per quart.	Pressure canner minutes at 10 lbs. (Pints)	Pressure canner minutes at 10 lbs. (Quarts)
Asparagus	Wash; trim off scales and tough ends; cut in 1-inch pieces. *Hot Pack:* Cook in boiling water 3 minutes; pack hot. Add salt, boiling cooking liquid: leave ½-inch headspace. Adjust lids; process. *Raw Pack:* Pack tightly into jars; add salt; cover with boiling water. Leave ½-inch headspace; adjust lids; process.	25 25	30 30
Beans Green and Wax	Wash; trim ends; cut in 1-inch pieces. *Hot Pack:* Cook 5 minutes in boiling water. Pack hot; add salt, hot cooking liquid; leave ½-inch headspace. Adjust lids; process. *Raw Pack:* Pack in jars; add salt; cover with boiling water. Leave ½-inch headspace; adjust lids; process.	20 20	25 25
Beans Lima	*Hot Pack:* Shell and wash young beans; cover with boiling water; bring to boil. Pack loosely to 1 inch from top of jar. Add salt and boiling water; leave 1-inch headspace; adjust lids; process. *Raw Pack:* Shell and wash young beans; pack loosely to 1 inch from top of pint jar, 1½ inches from top of quart jar. Add salt and boiling water; leave ½-inch headspace; adjust lids; process.	40 40	50 50
Beets	Wash, leaving on root and 1 inch of tops. Cover with boiling water; precook about 15 minutes. Slip off skins and trim; cube or slice large beets. Pack hot. Add salt and boiling water. Leave ½-inch headspace. Adjust lids; process.	30	35
Carrots	*Hot Pack:* Wash and pare; slice or dice. Cover with boiling water and bring to boil. Pack hot; add salt and boiling cooking liquid. Leave ½-inch headspace. Adjust lids; process. *Raw Pack:* Wash; pare; slice or dice. Pack tightly into jars; add salt, boiling water. Leave ½-inch headspace. Adjust lids, process.	25 25	30 30
Corn Whole kernel	Cut corn from cob; do not scrape cob. *Hot Pack:* Add 2 cups boiling water per 1 quart of corn; bring to boil. Pack hot corn loosely. Add salt and boiling hot cooking liquid leaving 1-inch headspace. Adjust lids; process. *Raw Pack:* Pack corn loosely to 1 inch from top. Add salt. Cover with boiling water leaving ½-inch headspace. Adjust lids; process.	55 55	85 85
Cream- style	Cut corn from cob, cutting only about half the kernel; scrape cob. *Hot Pack:* Follow directions above; pack hot corn in pints only. *Raw Pack:* Follow directions above except pack to 1½ inches from top of *pint* jars. Fill with boiling water; leave ½-inch headspace.	85 95	
Greens, all kinds	Wash thoroughly; cut out tough stems and midribs. Steam in cheese-cloth bag till well wilted, 10 minutes. Pack hot greens loosely. Add ¼ teaspoon salt to pints and ½ teaspoon salt to quarts; cover with boiling water. Leave ½-inch headspace; adjust lids; process.	70	90
Mushrooms	Wash thoroughly; trim stems. Slice, or leave small mushrooms whole. Steam 4 minutes or heat gently, covered, without liquid 15 minutes. Pack hot in pint jars; add ½ teaspoon salt per pint. For good color use ascorbic acid color keeper (follow label directions). Cover with boiling water. Leave ½-inch headspace; adjust lids; process.	30	
Peas Green	*Hot Pack:* Shell; wash. Cover with boiling water; bring to boil. Pack hot peas loosely to 1 inch from top of jar. Add salt and boiling water. Leave 1-inch headspace; adjust lids; process. *Raw Pack:* Shell and wash peas. Pack loosely to 1 inch from top of jar. Add salt; cover with boiling water leaving 1½-inches headspace. Adjust lids; process.	40 40	40 40

Potatoes New White	Wash; precook 10 minutes; remove skins. Pack hot; add salt; cover with boiling water. Leave ½-inch headspace. Adjust lids; process.	30	40
Sweet	*Dry Pack:* Wash; precook in boiling water 20 to 30 minutes. Remove skins; cut up. Pack hot to 1-inch from top; press gently; add no liquid or salt. Leave 1-inch headspace. Adjust lids; process.	65	95
	Wet Pack: Wash; boil till skins slip off easily. Remove skins; cut potatoes in pieces. Pack hot to 1-inch from top. Add salt. Cover with boiling water leaving 1-inch headspace. Adjust lids; process.	55	90
Pumpkin Squash Winter	Wash; remove seeds; pare and cube. Barely cover with water; bring to boil. Pack hot. Add salt; cover with boiling cooking liquid. Leave ½-inch headspace; adjust lids; process.	55	90
	Sieved pumpkin or squash: Wash; remove seeds. Pare and cut up. Steam about 25 minutes or till tender. Put through food mill or strainer. Heat through, stirring to prevent sticking. Pack hot. Add no liquid or salt. Leave ½-inch headspace; adjust lids; process.	65	80

Check jars for nicks and cracks before washing. Replace self-sealing lids; follow manufacturer's directions for cleaning.

Before covering, wipe jar rim with clean, damp cloth. Place lid with sealing compound down, next to glass; screw band tightly.

Use funnel to fill jars. For cold pack, cover vegetable with boiling water; leave headspace for expansion during processing.

11. To store jars, remove screw bands from two-piece metal lids. Wipe jars; label with contents and date. Store in a cool, dry, and dark place for up to one year.

To use vegetables, puncture metal disc and lift up. For zinc screw caps, pull out rubber ring, using pliers, before unscrewing the cap. Look for spoilage—leaks, bulging lids, spurting, or off odors. Never taste food with these signs. Even though spoilage may not be apparent, always boil corn and spinach 20 minutes before eating, and all other vegetables (except tomatoes) 10 minutes. Destroy food if an off-odor or foaming develops. (See *Jam, Jelly, Pickle* for additional information.)

To process meat or vegetables in pressure canner, arrange filled jars (not touching) in wire rack before placing in canner.

Lower jars on rack into canner containing 2 to 3 inches hot water. Follow manufacturer's directions for operating canner.

Stand jars apart and away from drafts to cool. To test seal, press down on center of lid. If lid is drawn down, jar is sealed.

Canning Tomatoes

Dip tomatoes in boiling water ½ minute; dip quickly in cold water. Remove stem ends; peel.

For raw pack: Pack tomatoes in jars; press gently to fill spaces. Leave ½-inch headspace. Add no water. Add 1 teaspoon salt to quarts. Adjust lids. Process in boiling water bath (see page 397, step 7), 35 minutes for pints or 45 minutes for quarts.

For hot pack: Quarter peeled tomatoes. Bring to boiling; stir constantly. Pack hot tomatoes into hot jars leaving ½-inch headspace. Add 1 teaspoon salt to quarts. Adjust lids. Process in boiling water bath (see page 397, step 7), 10 minutes for both pints and quarts.

For juice: Wash, remove stem ends, and cut tomatoes in pieces. Simmer until soft; stir often. Sieve. Add 1 teaspoon salt to each quart. Bring to boiling. Fill hot jars with hot juice leaving ½-inch headspace. Adjust lids. Process in boiling water bath (see page 397, step 7), 10 minutes for both pints and quarts.

Canned vegetable yield

Generally, for 1 quart canned vegetables prepare the following amount of fresh vegetable as picked or purchased:

Vegetable	Pounds
Asparagus	2½ to 4½
Beans, lima in pods	3 to 5
Beans, snap green	1½ to 2½
Beets, without tops	2 to 3½
Carrots, without tops	2 to 3
Corn, sweet in husks	3 to 6
Peas, green, in pods	3 to 6
Squash, winter	1½ to 3
Sweet potatoes	2 to 3
Tomatoes	2½ to 3½

CANTALOUPE, CANTALOUP, CANTALOPE, CANTELOPE—A member of the muskmelon family having a hard rind and a deep, apricot-colored flesh. Technically, the term cantaloupe should refer only to the hard rind variety of muskmelon. However, common usage has adopted the name to refer to the more popular netted variety.

Cantaloupe was named for the Castle of Cantalup, the home of a sixteenth century pope. It was in the Castle gardens that a variety of muskmelon brought from Armenia was first cultivated in Europe.

Cantaloupe was planted in the United States as early as 1609. However, no attempt was made to cultivate it commercially until near the close of the nineteenth century. Today, cantaloupe is produced commercially in 25 states with California being the leading producer.

Nutritional value: One-fourth of a five-inch cantaloupe supplies 30 calories while providing over two-thirds the daily adult requirement for vitamin A, and slightly less than half the daily requirement for vitamin C. Although other vitamins and minerals are present, they appear in much smaller amounts.

How to select: Cantaloupe is available throughout the year, but the largest supply appears on the market during the summer. Although a foolproof method for selecting a sweet, ripe, and juicy melon is

Captivate a summer luncheon with Cantaloupe Stars. To make bold zigzag edge, use a pencil to mark lines before cutting.

Uniformly shaped cantaloupe balls are simple to make with a melon-ball cutter. Serve alone or combine with other fresh fruits.

lacking, a few guides can be used as a fairly reliable indicator of quality.

A smooth calloused scar should be visible on the blossom end indicating the melon was mature when harvested, the netting should cover the melon thickly and stand out in bold relief, and it should have a dry, grayish color with the skin beneath the netting having a yellow tinge —too deep a yellow may indicate over-ripeness. Shape is another sign of quality; the rounder the melon, the sweeter the fruit. In addition, these are two other indications of maturity: there should be a delicate aroma at the blossom end, and a rattling of seeds in the melon when it is shaken.

How to store: If possible, plan to purchase melons a few days before using. Then, hold at room temperature two to three days. This allows the meat to soften and become juicy. However, if melons are ripe when purchased, they are best refrigerated to prevent over-ripening. Wash and dry melons. Wrap in moisture-vaporproof wrap, as the aroma of cantaloupe quickly penetrates other foods in the refrigerator.

How to use: A cantaloupe may be served in halves, wedges, slices, or balls. After cutting, remove all seeds and discard. The rind may or may not be removed.

Juicy melon balls peek from a fluffy lime filling in Seafoam Cantaloupe Pie. Top with whipped cream and sprinkle with toasted coconut for a cool and refreshing summertime dessert.

Served alone in the shell, cantaloupe makes an attractive breakfast fruit. Cut into balls, it is a refreshing addition to a fruit cup or salad. Cantaloupe à la mode features ice cream served in the hollow of the melon. (See also *Melon*.)

Tuna–Melon Dinner Salad

Combine 4 cups torn lettuce (½ large head); 2 cups cubed cantaloupe; one 11-ounce can mandarin oranges, drained; one 6½- or 7-ounce can tuna, drained and flaked; ¾ cup sliced process American cheese cut in strips; ½ cup chopped celery; ¼ cup sliced green onion; and ¼ cup sliced pitted ripe olives. Blend ½ cup mayonnaise and 1 tablespoon lemon juice; add to tuna mixture; toss. Makes 8 servings.

Cantaloupe Mist

Serve as a chilled, appetizer soup—

    1 large ripe cantaloupe
    ¼ teaspoon ground cinnamon
    1 6-ounce can frozen orange juice
        concentrate, thawed
    2 juice cans water
    2 tablespoons lime juice
      Lime wedges *or* mint sprigs

Halve melon; remove seeds and discard. Scoop out pulp. In blender container, combine melon pulp and cinnamon. Blend till puréed. Mix orange juice concentrate, water, and lime juice. Add melon purée. Chill. Serve in individual ice jackets; garnish each serving with lime wedge or mint sprig. Makes 6 cups.

Seafoam Cantaloupe Pie

    1 envelope unflavored gelatin
        (1 tablespoon)
    ½ cup sugar
    ¼ teaspoon salt
    4 slightly beaten egg yolks
    ½ cup lime juice
    1 teaspoon grated lime peel
      Few drops green food coloring
    4 egg whites
    ½ cup sugar
    ½ cup whipping cream
    1½ cups cantaloupe balls
    1 *baked* 9-inch pastry shell,
        cooled (*See Pastry*)

Combine first 3 ingredients. Blend egg yolks, lime juice, and ¼ cup water; add to gelatin mixture. Cook and stir over medium heat just till mixture comes to boiling. Remove from heat; add lime peel and food coloring. Chill, stirring occasionally, till mixture mounds.

Beat egg whites to soft peaks; gradually add ½ cup sugar. Beat to stiff peaks. Fold in gelatin mixture. Whip cream; fold in whipped cream and cantaloupe. Pile into cooled pastry shell. Chill till firm. Top with additional whipped cream and toasted coconut, if desired.

Cantaloupe Stars

Stand a large cantaloupe on end. To cut zigzag edge, push sharp knife into center at an angle; pull out and make next cut at opposite angle (see picture, page 401). Repeat around melon. Pull halves apart; remove seeds.

Fill centers with a mixture of fresh fruits—strawberries, raspberries, pitted cherries or grapes, melon balls, or pineapple chunks. Drizzle thawed frozen lemonade concentrate over fruit. Chill. Makes 2 servings.

CANTONESE-STYLE COOKERY—A method of food preparation adapted from the cuisine of Canton, China and the surrounding area. (See also *Oriental Cookery*.)

CANVASBACK DUCK—A wild bird of North America prized for its flavor when roasted. It is named for the grayish, canvaslike appearance on its back. (See also *Duck*.)

CAPER—The flavor bud of the caper bush which is used to season or garnish food. Sometimes called "mountain pepper," the caper plant grows wild—mostly in dry, rocky places, from the Mediterranean to India. Bearing somewhat large, but short-lived white blossoms with purplish-stalked stamens, it is cultivated in the United States only for its decorative value.

The French variety of capers is considered superior to all others, including the English caper. The best capers are perfectly round, very small, and quite firm. Their flavor is pungent and slightly bitter. However, they should not be confused with pickled nasturtium seeds which are larger than caper buds, yet sometimes served as a substitute for capers.

Capers are most often pickled in vinegar and bottled, although sometimes they are available packed in salt. They are used frequently in the cuisine of many European as well as Southeast Asian countries. In the United States, imported pickled capers are most often used to garnish or add a flavor accent to hot and cold sauces, vegetables, salads, and meat dishes.

Caper Burgers

    ¼ cup butter or margarine
    1 tablespoon drained capers
            •   •   •
    1½ pounds ground beef
    1 teaspoon salt
      Dash pepper
      Kitchen bouquet
    4 thick slices French bread,
        toasted and buttered

Blend butter with capers. Form into 4 patties, ½ inch thick; turn out on waxed paper. Freeze till firm. Combine beef, salt, and pepper; shape into four 2-inch-thick oval patties, the size of French bread slices. Make depression in center of each, pressing down to ½ inch from bottom. Place frozen caper-butter patty in each depression. Mold meat to cover butter.

Brush with kitchen bouquet. Broil over *medium-hot* coals for 10 minutes. Turn carefully (so butter doesn't leak out) and broil 10 minutes more. Beef will be rare next to butter. Serve on toasted French bread. Makes 4 servings.

Jacques' Chicken Salad

    1 10-ounce package frozen
          French-style green beans,
          cooked and drained, *or* 1
          16-ounce can green beans, drained
    ¼ cup Italian salad dressing
    3 large chicken breasts, cooked,
          boned, and chilled
    ¼ cup whipping cream
    ½ cup mayonnaise
    1 cup diced celery
    3 lettuce cups
          Mayonnaise or salad dressing
    2 teaspoons drained capers
    6 tomato slices
    6 ripe olives
    2 hard-cooked eggs, quartered

Combine beans and Italian dressing. Chill several hours; stir occasionally. Cut 3 thin slices from chicken breasts and reserve. Cube remaining chicken. Whip cream. Gently fold the ½ cup mayonnaise into whipped cream.

Fold cubed chicken, celery, ½ teaspoon salt, and dash pepper into mayonnaise mixture. Chill thoroughly. Place lettuce cups on serving platter. Fill with chicken mixture. Top with reserved chicken slices and dollop of mayonnaise; sprinkle with capers. Drain beans; arrange between salads. Garnish with tomato slices, olives, and egg wedges. Makes 3 servings.

Caper Mayonnaise

Combine 1 cup mayonnaise or salad dressing; ¼ cup drained capers, coarsely chopped; 3 tablespoons chopped onion; and 2 tablespoons chopped toasted almonds. Serve warm or chilled over fish or vegetables. Makes 1½ cups.

CAPON *(kā' pon, -puhn)*—A rooster which has been castrated. When marketed, capons weigh from four to seven pounds. They provide a generous amount of white meat and fine flavor when roasted. (See also *Chicken.*)

An elegant salad for a special luncheon—Jacques' Chicken Salad. Capers dot chicken-capped salad served with marinated green beans, tomato slices, olives, and hard-cooked eggs.

Breast of Capon Isabelle

6 breasts of capon, boned,
    skinned, and split lengthwise
2 tablespoons butter or margarine
2½ cups chicken stock

   •   •   •

1 pound fine noodles
2 tablespoons butter or margarine

   •   •

1 pint fresh mushrooms, sliced
    (about 2 cups sliced)
¼ cup butter or margarine
¼ cup dry white wine
½ teaspoon salt
  Dash pepper
2 tablespoons all-purpose flour

   •   •   •

¼ cup butter or margarine
¼ cup all-purpose flour
1 teaspoon salt
2 cups light cream
3 slightly beaten egg yolks

In large skillet brown breasts in 2 tablespoons butter. Add *2 tablespoons* of the chicken stock. Cover; cook 30 minutes or till tender.

Meanwhile, cook noodles in boiling, salted water till tender; drain. Toss lightly with 2 tablespoons butter; keep hot.

Cook mushrooms in ¼ cup butter with wine, ½ teaspoon salt, and dash pepper till tender, about 5 minutes. Sprinkle with 2 tablespoons flour; stir to blend. Keep warm.

Remove breasts from skillet; keep warm. In same skillet, melt ¼ cup butter; blend in ¼ cup flour, 1 teaspoon salt, and dash pepper. Add remaining chicken stock and cream all at once. Cook and stir till mixture thickens and bubbles. Remove from heat; stir a little hot mixture into egg yolks. Return to hot mixture. Continue cooking, stirring constantly, just till mixture boils. Remove from heat.

Serve capon breasts on hot buttered noodles; top with mushroom mixture. Pour cream sauce over all. Makes 8 to 12 servings.

CAPPUCCINO *(kap′ ŏo chē′ nō, kä pŏo-)*—An Italian beverage prepared with espresso coffee and milk or whipping cream and served hot. Often it is served with a sprinkling of cinnamon and a cinnamon stick stirrer. (See also *Beverage*.)

Rich, dark espresso topped with whipped cream becomes an Italian favorite—Cappuccino. Serve with cinnamon stick stirrers.

Cappuccino

¼ cup instant espresso coffee
    or instant coffee powder
½ cup whipping cream, whipped
    Ground cinnamon *or* ground
      nutmeg
    Cinnamon stick stirrers

Dissolve coffee in 2 cups boiling water; pour into cups. Top each cup with spoonful of whipped cream; dash with cinnamon *or* nutmeg. Serve with cinnamon stick stirrers. Pass sugar, if desired. Makes 6 or 7 small servings.

CAPSICUM *(kap′ suh kuhm)*—Any one of a number of pod-bearing plants native to tropical America. The many-seeded peppers borne by the numerous Capsicum varieties vary in size, color, and shape.

The Capsicum family may be divided into two classes—sweet and hot. Among the sweet is the bell or green pepper, most often used fresh. The hot varieties range from mildly warm to extremely hot, and include pimientos, chilies, and bird peppers. Sometimes used fresh, hot peppers most often are dried in the preparation of various seasonings such as chili powder, red pepper, cayenne, and paprika.

CAQUELON—A French earthenware casserole traditionally used for cheese fondue.

CARAMEL *(kar' uh muhl)*—1. A syrup made by cooking granulated sugar until it melts and changes color. 2. A rich chewy candy.

Caramel, the golden brown syrup, is used to flavor desserts, stews, and gravies. It is also known as burnt sugar.

Caramel candies are made with milk, butter and sugar. They are cut into cubes for serving. Commercial caramels come in butterscotch or chocolate flavors and in individual wraps. These caramels are used as candy or as an ingredient when melted with a liquid. (See also *Candy*.)

Caramels

    1 cup butter or margarine
    1 pound brown sugar (2¼ cups)
    1 cup light corn syrup
    1 15-ounce can sweetened
       condensed milk
    1 teaspoon vanilla

Melt butter or margarine in heavy 3-quart saucepan. Add sugar and dash salt; stir thoroughly. Stir in corn syrup; mix well. Gradually add milk, stirring constantly. Cook and stir over medium heat to firm-ball stage (245°), 12 to 15 minutes. Remove from heat; stir in vanilla. Pour into buttered 9x9x2-inch pan. Cool and cut candy into squares.

Caramel Cakewiches

    1 2-ounce package dessert
       topping mix
    1 large banana, sliced
    ½ 14-ounce package vanilla
       caramels (about 1½ cups)
    1 6-ounce can evaporated milk
       (⅔ cup)
    3 to 4 drops bitters
    6 slices pound cake

Prepare dessert topping mix according to package directions; fold in the sliced banana. Chill. In medium saucepan combine caramels and evaporated milk. Cook and stir over medium heat till caramels are melted; stir in bitters. To serve, top pound cake slices with banana mixture, then pour the warm caramel sauce over cakewich. Makes 6 servings.

CARAMELIZE—To change into caramel. Caramelizing is the process (1) of cooking granulated sugar until it melts, (2) of coating food with caramel, (3) of coating food with sugar and then cooking, or (4) of coating a mold or baking dish with caramel before adding the batter or food.

CARAWAY—An aromatic herb of the parsley family which has a tangy, pungent flavor. The caraway plant reaches the height of two feet and has green, feathery leaves and white flowers. The brown seeds are small (about three-sixteenths of an inch in length), curved, and tapered.

Caraway is an ancient herb. It was originally grown in the Caria region of Asia Minor from which the name caraway is derived. Roman soldiers brought the herb from Asia 2,000 years ago, thus helping it spread over all of their known world.

Caraway soon became popular as both a seasoning and a medicine. It developed as a distinctive part of German, English, Austrian, and Hungarian cookery. Used early as a medicine, it was credited with such feats as curing hysteria and restoring hair to the bald. Today, its value in medicines is still recognized.

The majority of caraway sold is imported from the Netherlands. However, it is cultivated in various parts of the United States, primarily in Maine. Whole caraway seed is the most common form of the herb found in the market and used for seasoning. These seeds can be stored for many years and not lose their aroma.

The entire caraway plant can be used for food. The fleshy root is cooked and eaten as a vegetable. The leaves, milder flavored than the seeds, are used to season soups, vegetables, and pork. Oil extracted from the seeds is a principle ingredient in the liqueur "kümmel."

You can use caraway seed as a seasoning in sauerkraut, coleslaw, stew, pork, bread, cookies, cheese, and vegetables. Rye bread's particular flavor comes from caraway. Caraway also gives a flavor-lift to carrots, spinach, or potato salad. Caraway is good combined with apple and can be used in many apple dishes. Also, caraway seed is good to munch after dinner, an ancient custom. (See also *Herb*.)

Austrian Cabbage Salad

      1 small head cabbage, shredded
         (6 cups)
      2 tablespoons salad oil
      2 tablespoons white wine vinegar
      2 tablespoons chopped green onion
    ½ teaspoon caraway seed
    ¼ teaspoon dried marjoram
         leaves, crushed
    ½ teaspoon salt
         Dash pepper
                • • •
      2 tablespoons snipped parsley
      1 tomato

Place cabbage in bowl; cover with boiling water. Let stand 5 minutes; drain well. To the cabbage add oil, vinegar, onion, caraway seed, marjoram, salt, and pepper. Toss; chill thoroughly. Just before serving, sprinkle salad with parsley. Cut tomato in wedges and place atop salad. Makes 6 servings.

Caraway Cookies

      1 cup butter or margarine
      1 cup sugar
      2 beaten eggs
   2¾ cups sifted all-purpose flour
      1 teaspoon baking soda
    ½ teaspoon cream of tartar
         Dash salt
    ½ cup chopped mixed candied
         fruits and peels
    ½ cup light raisins
      2 tablespoons caraway seed
      2 tablespoons rose water *or* water

Cream butter, sugar, and eggs till fluffy. Sift together flour, soda, cream of tartar, and salt; add to creamed mixture. Stir in candied fruits and peels, raisins, caraway seed, and water. Drop from teaspoon onto ungreased cookie sheet. Flatten with glass dipped in flour; center each with a light raisin. Bake at 375° for 8 to 10 minutes. Cool on rack. Makes 4½ dozen.

Caraway seed lends a pungent flavor and nutlike texture to cabbage. Try it in slaw, such as Austrian Cabbage Salad.

Caraway Fingers

6 frankfurter rolls
¼ cup garlic spread
¼ cup butter or margarine
¼ cup grated Parmesan cheese
2 teaspoons caraway seed

Quarter rolls lengthwise. Melt garlic spread and butter; brush on cut sides of rolls. Sprinkle with cheese, then caraway seed. Bake on cookie sheet at 450° for 5 to 8 minutes.

Caraway Chicken Halves

½ cup salad oil
¼ cup light corn syrup
¼ cup chopped onion
1 tablespoon lemon juice
1 teaspoon dried oregano leaves, crushed
1 teaspoon caraway seed
2 2- to 2½-pound ready-to-cook broiler-fryer chickens, halved lengthwise

Combine first 6 ingredients and ½ teaspoon salt. Brush over chicken halves. Place chicken halves on grill, bone side down. Broil over *slow* coals 25 minutes; turn, broil 20 minutes, brushing occasionally with herb mixture. Continue broiling, till meat is tender, about 10 minutes, turning occasionally and brushing with herb mixture. Makes 4 servings.

Caraway, identified by the feathery leaves and white flowers, is an attractive and useful herb to include in a home garden.

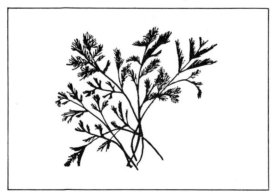

CARBOHYDRATE—A class of foods including sugars, starches, and cellulose. Sugars and starches provide energy for growth, maintenance, and activities of the body. Cellulose adds bulk to the diet.

Natural sources of carbohydrates are fruits, vegetables, milk, and cereals. Sugar is found in fruits, milk, and many vegetables. Rice, corn, potatoes, and wheat have a high starch content. Only a few foods, such as cane and beet sugar and cornstarch, are entirely made of carbohydrates. Some of these foods or foods made with them, such as bread and ice cream, should be eaten each day.

CARBONATED BEVERAGE—A drink which bubbles or fizzes because it has been charged with carbon dioxide under pressure. Many of these beverages are flavored with syrups, cola, and aromatic root.

Carbonated beverages are used as an ingredient with other foods as well as for chilled drinks served alone. They add sparkle and flavor to many gelatin salads, fruit punches, ice cream sodas, fruit sauces, dips, and desserts. They are also good as mixers for alcoholic beverages.

Once a container has been opened it should be tightly covered to keep the carbon dioxide from escaping for this causes a flat taste. (See also *Beverage*.)

Golden Glow Punch

1 3-ounce package orange-flavored gelatin
1 6-ounce can frozen pineapple-orange juice concentrate
4 cups apple juice
1 28-ounce bottle ginger ale, chilled (3½ cups)

Dissolve gelatin in 1 cup *boiling* water. Stir in pineapple-orange concentrate. Add apple juice and 3 cups cold water. Carefully pour in chilled ginger ale. Makes about 25 four-ounce servings of Golden Glow Punch.

CARBON DIOXIDE—A colorless, odorless gas. Carbon dioxide performs many functions in cooking. Baked foods are leavened

Pour carbonated beverages carefully down the *side* of glass just before serving to save those bubbles which give sparkle and zing.

by the carbon dioxide bubbles which are produced during the reaction of baking soda or baking powder and an acid. Carbon dioxide is also formed during fermentation and makes bubbles in beer and some wine. Carbonated beverages are bubbly because of this gas. Dry ice, its solid form, is often used to preserve foods.

CARDAMOM, CARDAMON (*kar' duh muhm*)
—A spice which tastes similar to anise and is sweeter than ginger. Its odor is pungent and sweet. Cardamom pods are the fruit of a plant of the ginger family. Each pod contains 17 to 20 tiny, black seeds.

This spice has been used for centuries in Indian and Scandinavian cookery. It may seem strange that two such distant countries share a love for the same spice. But the explanation is simple: cardamom is native to India and was discovered there by Vikings who took it to their countries 1,000 years ago. Cardamom is a traditional flavor in typical Indian dishes, such as curry, and in typical Danish pastries.

Cardamom is recognized as the world's second most precious spice. (Saffron is first.) It's expensive to produce since an acre yields only 250 pounds of the pods and each pod must be snipped from the plant by hand with scissors.

Whole pods, whole seeds, and ground cardamom are available. When recipes call for crushed cardamom, either the whole pod or whole seed can be used. Remove the outer soft shell if using pods; grind the seed to a powder with a mortar and pestle or crush with two tablespoons.

Cardamom awakens and accents the flavor of main dishes, orange slices, melons, jellies, fruit salads, and pastries, especially Christmas pastries. When flavoring with the spice, use the exact amount called for in the recipe, or add sparingly since it is quite pungent. (See also *Spice*.)

Cardamom Cookies

> 1 **cup sifted all-purpose flour**
> ½ **cup granulated sugar**
> ⅛ **or** ¼ **teaspoon ground cardamom**
>   **Dash ground cinnamon**
> ¼ **teaspoon shredded lemon peel**
> ¼ **cup ground almonds**
> 6 **tablespoons butter or margarine**
> 1 **beaten egg**
> 2 **teaspoons milk**
>   **Granulated sugar**

Sift together flour, sugar, cardamom, and cinnamon; stir in peel and almonds. Cut in butter till mixture resembles coarse crumbs. Stir in egg and milk till mixture forms a ball; chill.

Roll out to about ⅛-inch thickness. Cut into circles 1¾ inches in diameter. Place on ungreased cookie sheet; sprinkle with sugar. Bake at 400° till edges are brown, about 6 to 8 minutes. Makes about 7 dozen.

Crush whole cardamom seeds by removing the outer soft shell, placing in a tablespoon, and crushing with back of a second spoon.

CARDOON *(kär dōōn')*—A silvery green, thistlelike plant. Although it's related to the globe artichoke, cardoon looks more like celery. The flavor of cardoon is similar to both celery and artichoke.

Cardoon leaves and stalk are a popular vegetable in Europe, especially in the Mediterranean regions. To prepare it, cut into short pieces, boil in salted water till tender-crisp, and then chill. Eat with dressing, use in salads or soups, serve hot in a sauce with veal, or coat in batter and fry. (See also *Vegetable*.)

CARIBOU *(kar' uh bōō)*—A large North American deer related to reindeer of Europe and Asia. (See also *Game*.)

CAROTENE *(kar' uh tēn')*—Yellow and orange pigments in plants that the body converts into vitamin A when eaten.

Carotene is found in fruits and vegetables that are bright yellow and dark green. (The green color is due to chlorophyll which dominates the color of yellow carotene.) Rich sources are carrots, sweet potatoes, green pepper, and spinach.

An exception to the rule that carotene-rich foods are either yellow or dark green is some red foods. For example, watermelon, tomato, pink grapefruit, apricot, and persimmons are rich in carotene.

A few animal foods are natural sources of carotene or have carotene added. Milk, egg yolk, and butter have this pigment which gives them a yellow color. Sometimes the pigment is extracted from vegetables and added to butter or cheese for additional color as well as nutrition.

Each day adults and teen-agers need 5,000 International Units of vitamin A, either the vitamin itself or carotene which will be converted into the vitamin. Small children need about half this amount.

Carotene is necessary for normal growth and good eyesight. When converted to vitamin A, it keeps the skin, the lining of the respiratory and digestive tracts, and the surface of the eyes in a healthy condition. Certain symptoms indicate a deficiency of carotene. These are eye diseases, night blindness, low resistance to infection, slow growth, poor tooth enamel, and loss of reproductive power. However, an excessive intake over a long period of time causes carotenemia, a harmless condition with the spectacular effect of giving the skin a somewhat yellowish hue.

Carotene is quite stable. It's not soluble in water, nor is it destroyed by acid, alkali, or heat. Therefore, carotene is seldom lost during the process of cooking a food. (See also *Vitamin*.)

CARP—A large, freshwater fish. They are a gold to olive color, about two feet long, and can weigh as much as 40 pounds. Carp are hardy. They adapt to new locations easily, survive in waters unsuited for other fish, and live 20 to 40 years.

The carp is an immigrant. It moved from China to Europe, and then in 1876, it was brought to America from Germany.

Carp provides food and sport to some fishermen. Its roe can be made into a pseudo-caviar. Properly prepared, the firm, lean flesh is a flavorful food. Fillets or whole fish, ranging from two to seven pounds, are baked, broiled, fried, or stewed. They are good prepared in beer.

The better quality carp are caught in cold water. Therefore, November to April are the best months to buy or to catch and use fresh carp for food. Those available during the summer months may have a slightly muddy flavor. (See also *Fish*.)

CARRAGEEN *(kar' uh gēn)*—An edible seaweed, also called Irish moss. Carrageen is stubby and dark purple in color. It grows along the coast of Ireland.

Eat carregeen in the dried form or use it to thicken foods, such as pudding.

CARROT—A long, tapering, yellowish root. Both the root and feathery leaves of this vegetable are edible. As a member of the parsley family, it's related to dill, parsnip, Queen Ann's Lace, and deadly hemlock.

It was first grown, as history records, in Afghanistan and adjacent regions. Chinese, Japanese, and Indians are known to have used it for food in the thirteenth century. As the carrot spread into Europe, the people not only enjoyed it as a vegetable, but also found some additional uses. For instance, the Germans finely chopped and browned carrots for a coffee substitute. Then when the vegetable was introduced from Holland, English women adorned their hair with its feathery leaves.

Finally, in 1609, carrots were brought to the Americas. Virginia was the first colony known to have grown them, but soon other colonies and the American Indians were also cultivating this crop. Today, California, Texas, Michigan, Arizona, and Florida are the major areas where carrots are grown in the United States.

Nutritional value: Carrots are rich in carotene as the name suggests. When eaten, carotene is converted into vitamin A by the body. An average raw carrot or one-third cup of cooked carrots gives the day's requirement of vitamin A. Each raw carrot supplies about 21 calories.

Eating raw carrots is excellent for dental health. Chewing on this crisp vegetable exercises the teeth, gums, and jaw muscles and helps to clean the teeth.

How to select: The most abundant selection of fresh carrots is available during the months of January to June. However, fresh, frozen, and canned carrots are usually plentiful throughout the year.

Select fresh carrots that are firm, well-shaped, smooth, clean, and dark in color. Carrots which are shriveled or soft lack flavor. Large, chubby carrots with cracks are likely to be overgrown and fibrous. The darker the color, the more carotene it contains, so choose the brightest yellow and golden ones available. If you buy carrots with tops still on, be certain the leaves appear fresh and bright green.

Select young, small carrots which are more tender and milder flavored for eating raw. Older, larger ones are suitable for cooking and for shredding.

Fresh carrots are sold with or without tops in bundles and in plastic bags. Packages vary in weight, but figure a one pound package to make three servings.

Frozen and canned carrots are available in many forms. The consumer can choose diced, sliced, shoestring, or whole carrots. Frozen carrots with a brown sugar glaze or a butter sauce and carrot juice are additional selections which can be found in most grocery stores and supermarkets.

How to store: Fresh carrots will keep from one to four weeks when stored correctly. Remove any tops which are still attached to carrots as soon as possible. The tops reduce the quality of the carrot if left on, for they draw out moisture and nutrients. Before putting away, rinse the carrots and cover with foil, waxed paper, clean plastic wrap, or a plastic bag. Store in a cool, moist place. The crisper of the refrigerator or a cool basement, where air circulates, are good locations for storage.

Freeze or can fresh carrots for longer storage. Blanch, package, and freeze carrots; use within a year. (See *Canning* for additional ways to preserve carrots).

How to prepare: Remove skin from the carrots by thinly scraping with a vegetable peeler. If desired, scrub young carrots with a stiff brush to remove the skin.

To cook the carrots, leave whole, dice, slice, or shred. Place in a saucepan which contains 1 inch of boiling, salted water. Cover the saucepan and cook till tender. Shredded carrots will take about 5 minutes, small pieces about 10 to 20, and whole carrots about 15 to 20. Season the carrots, add butter or margarine, and use as is or as an ingredient in a recipe.

How to use: Carrots fit into every course in the menu. Appetizers of carrot juice, carrot soup, carrot curls on a relish tray, or carrot sticks for dips are colorful as well as stimulating to the appetite.

Salads are enhanced by crisp, cold, sweet bits of carrot. Raisins and carrots are a popular salad combination. Carrot slices and shreds are quite good in both tossed and gelatin salad recipes.

Pineapple-Carrot Toss

    1 8¾-ounce can pineapple
        tidbits, drained
    2 cups shredded carrots
    ½ cup plumped raisins
        Mayonnaise or salad dressing

Combine pineapple, carrots, and raisins. Chill thoroughly. Just before serving, add mayonnaise to moisten. Makes 6 servings.

Carrots frequently appear in the main dish of the menu. Casseroles and soufflés use them as a main ingredient or as a complementary flavor to the main food. Carrots and potatoes are traditionally cooked with pot roast. Garnishes of carrot zigzags, curls, and corkscrews are attractive on the main dish. Both the root and leaves can be used in stew.

Burgundy Beef Stew

      1 10¾-ounce can condensed
            tomato soup
      1 10½-ounce can condensed beef
            broth
      ½ cup red Burgundy
      3 tablespoons all-purpose flour
      ½ teaspoon dried basil leaves,
            crushed

· · ·

   1½ pounds beef chuck, cut in
            1-inch cubes
      4 medium potatoes, peeled and
            halved
      4 medium carrots, quartered
      1 large onion, sliced

In a large saucepan combine tomato soup, beef broth, and Burgundy; blend in flour, 1 teaspoon salt, dash pepper, and basil. Add meat, potatoes, carrots, and onion; stir to distribute through gravy. Cover and simmer 1½ hours, stirring occasionally. Makes 6 servings.

As a side-dish vegetable in the main course, carrots go well with all meats. Simply boil the vegetable and season with salt and pepper—or with other herbs and spices, such as parsley, thyme, dill, cloves, ginger, mint, rosemary, and garlic. These add a different flavor combination. Carrots can be baked, mashed, glazed with honey or seasoned with lemon butter.

Bright, golden carrots

←Include vitamin-rich carrots in menus for their crisp texture, color, and sweet flavor. Raw or cooked they are low in calories.

Minted Carrots

      5 or 6 carrots
      2 tablespoons butter or margarine
      1 tablespoon honey
      2 teaspoons chopped fresh mint

Cut carrots in strips, cook in boiling salted water till tender, and drain. Combine butter or margarine, honey, and mint; heat till butter is melted. Add carrots; simmer till glazed, about 8 minutes. Makes 4 or 5 servings.

Desserts made from carrots are becoming more and more popular. Delicious cakes, pies, and puddings use carrots as a major ingredient for flavor and texture. Carrots are also great for nibbling between meals. (See also *Vegetable*.)

Carrot-Pineapple Cake

   1½ cups sifted all-purpose flour
      1 cup sugar
      1 teaspoon baking powder
      1 teaspoon baking soda
      1 teaspoon ground cinnamon
      ⅔ cup salad oil
      2 eggs
      1 cup finely shredded carrot
      ½ cup crushed pineapple
            (with syrup)
      1 teaspoon vanilla
         Cream Cheese Frosting

Sift together into large mixing bowl flour, sugar, baking powder, soda, cinnamon, and ½ teaspoon salt. Add salad oil, eggs, carrot, pineapple, and vanilla. Mix till moistened; beat 2 minutes at medium speed on electric mixer.

Bake in greased and floured 9x9x2-inch pan at 350° about 35 minutes. Cool 10 minutes; remove from pan. Cool. Frost.

Cream Cheese Frosting: In small mixing bowl combine one 3-ounce package cream cheese, softened; 1 tablespoon butter or margarine, softened; and 1 teaspoon vanilla. Beat at low speed on electric mixer till light. Gradually add 2 cups sifted confectioners' sugar, beating till fluffy. If necessary, add milk to make of spreading consistency. Stir in ½ cup chopped pecans, if desired. Frosts one 9-inch cake.

Parslied Carrots

8 medium carrots
2 tablespoons water
2 tablespoons butter or margarine
1 teaspoon sugar
¼ teaspoon salt
Dash pepper
2 teaspoons snipped parsley

Peel carrots; halve lengthwise. Place in 10x6x 1½-inch baking dish. Add water, butter or margarine, sugar, salt, and pepper. Cover tightly with foil. Bake at 400° till tender, about 45 to 50 minutes. Sprinkle with parsley before serving. Makes 4 to 6 servings.

Skillet Carrots

Melt 3 tablespoons butter in skillet. Add 8 medium carrots, coarsely shredded. Sprinkle with ½ teaspoon salt. Cover and cook till tender, 5 to 8 minutes. Top with snipped parsley.

Sprinkle snipped parsley over baked carrots to dress up a vegetable dish. Parslied Carrots are suitable for oven meal menus.

Spicy Carrot Sticks

2 tablespoons butter or margarine
1 teaspoon cornstarch
½ cup water
4 whole cloves
2 bay leaves
8 medium carrots, cut in thin
  strips (about 4 cups)

Melt butter in saucepan and blend in cornstarch. Add water. Cook, stirring constantly, until mixture is thickened. Add 1 teaspoon salt, dash pepper, cloves, bay leaves, and carrots. Cover pan and simmer till carrots are tender, about 10 to 12 minutes. Remove cloves and bay leaves. Makes 6 servings.

Golden Carrot Bake

3 cups shredded carrots
2 cups cooked rice
6 ounces process American
  cheese, shredded (1½ cups)
½ cup milk
2 beaten eggs
2 tablespoons minced onion
1 teaspoon salt
¼ teaspoon pepper
2 ounces process American
  cheese, shredded (½ cup)

Combine carrots, rice, 1½ cups cheese, milk, and eggs. Stir in onion, salt, and pepper. Pour mixture into a greased 1½-quart casserole dish. Sprinkle the ½ cup cheese over top. Bake at 350° for 50 to 60 minutes. Makes 6 servings.

Carrots Supreme

1 tablespoon butter or margarine
1 cup sliced carrots
1 cup bias-sliced celery
½ cup green pepper strips
Dash dried dillweed

Melt butter in heavy skillet; add carrots, celery, and green pepper. Cover and cook over medium heat 7 minutes. Season with ½ teaspoon salt, dash pepper, and dillweed. Cook over low heat till vegetables are just tender, about 5 minutes. Makes 3 or 4 servings.

Carrots Lyonnaise

Made with a French flair—

1 pound carrots (6 medium)
1 chicken bouillon cube
½ cup boiling water

. . .

¼ cup butter or margarine
3 medium onions, sliced
1 tablespoon all-purpose flour
¼ teaspoon salt
  Dash pepper
¾ cup water
  Sugar

Peel carrots and cut in julienne strips. Dissolve bouillon cube in the ½ cup boiling water. Cook carrots in bouillon, covered, 10 minutes. In saucepan melt butter; add onions and cook, covered, 15 minutes, stirring occasionally. Stir in flour, salt, pepper, and the ¾ cup water; bring to boiling. Add carrots and bouillon; simmer, uncovered, 10 minutes. Add pinch of sugar. Makes 6 servings.

Summertime Carrots

2 cups sliced carrots
¼ cup beef broth
1 teaspoon cornstarch
2 tablespoons sauterne
1 cup seedless green grapes
1 tablespoon butter or margarine
½ teaspoon lemon juice
¼ teaspoon salt

Cook carrots in beef broth till crisp-tender, 8 to 10 minutes. Blend cornstarch with sauterne; stir into carrots. Add grapes, butter, lemon juice, salt, and dash pepper. Cook and stir just till mixture comes to boiling. Serves 4.

Glazed Carrots

In skillet heat ⅓ cup brown sugar and 2 tablespoons butter till sugar dissolves. Add 8 cooked carrots (whole or halved lengthwise); cook over medium heat, turning carrots till well glazed and tender, about 12 minutes.

Dramatize vegetables with a smidgen of sugar, a tang of orange, or a hint of onion. Fine examples are Carrots Lyonnaise and Orange-Glazed Baby Beets. (See *Beet* for recipe.)

CARVING —Cutting meat, fish, or poultry into slices or pieces for serving.

Carving was one of the first dining arts to be refined. From ancient Roman days until the Elizabethan era, men of high rank were the official carvers. However, for a short period, women did do some of the carving as well as other hostess chores. The idea of paper frills on poultry and meat is a direct carry-over from those days when they were used to protect the lady's fingers from greasy meat. This woman's role, however, soon reverted back to the men. Today, carving is considered the man's domain, although it's quite acceptable for women to carve.

Carving serves an important function for both the food and the dining atmosphere. Meat correctly carved, is more attractive and more appetizing. The flavor is better because the juices do not flow out. More servings are available with less waste —making the meat more economical.

A dramatic atmosphere can be achieved by carving at the table. This is a ceremony which the host can rightfully be proud to perform and guests honored to witness.

However, if the host is carving and he is not experienced or confident in his carving abilities, the hostess should carry on a conversation with the guests. This will help divert some of the attention away from the carver while he carves.

Basic equipment: For carving, one needs the food, platter, knife, fork, and steel.

The meat must be properly prepared. Have the meatman saw the bones, especially the backbone, or remove the bones entirely. The absence of bones simplifies the job. Do not overcook the meat or it will fall apart when you slice. Let a roast stand 10 to 20 minutes before carving so the meat can firm up. It's not necessary to let steaks and chops stand. Cover the roast loosely with a piece of foil to keep it warm. Remove strings and skewers. However, leave a few strings on a rolled roast so it won't unroll when carved.

Place the meat on a platter which is suitable for carving. A wooden one is best since it does not dull the knife. Also, there are specially designed platters with spikes to hold the meat in place.

Sharp knives are essential for easy carving. Select an electric knife or standard hollow-ground knife with a sturdy well-riveted handle. Choose a knife or set for its good blade and construction rather than for decorative handles. Use a fork to hold meat steady while cutting. Some forks even have guards which protect the hand. The tines are sharp and vary in width for the intended purpose.

You need several knives and forks for carving: (1) An 11-inch knife with a straight edge and narrow blade and a fork with wide tines for a large roast, ham, sirloin, or rib roast. (2) An eight- or nine-inch knife with curved blade, and a fork with narrow tines, for medium and small roasts and legs of lamb. (3) A six- or seven-inch curved-edge knife and a fork with narrow tines for steaks, chops, and poultry.

You also need a steel or another knife sharpener to keep the blade true and sharp.

Basic techniques: The stage must be set properly for easy carving, whether it be done in the kitchen or at the table.

The carver must know the anatomy of the meat—the location of the bones and how the grain runs. Striking a bone accidentally dulls the knife and can possibly knock over the meat. The cutting is usually done across grain. (Grain is the long fibers.) Cutting across the grain makes meat easier to chew and juicier. But when grain is not easy to determine, follow the meatman's original cut.

Arrange the meat on a platter which is large enough to hold it and the slices— or provide another plate for the slices. Avoid excessive garnishes or vegetables on the meat platter which can get in the way or get knocked off during carving.

Now you can (as the carver) begin the ceremony which, of course, has been well rehearsed before presenting before guests. Sharpen the knife with the steel, firmly insert the fork, and slice with steady, firm strokes. Keep the knife angle the same so the slices will be uniform. Stack slices until enough is carved for one round of servings. This keeps the slices warm during carving. Place servings on warmed plates. Don't forget to divide and serve garnishes, vegetables, or stuffings, also.

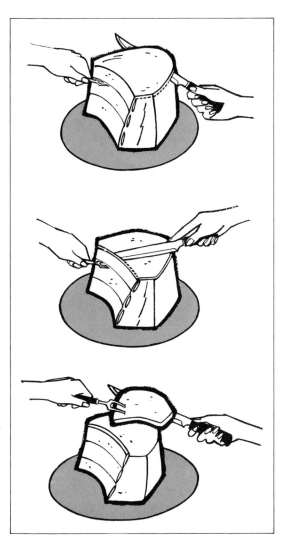

Flank steak, *below*, is held on board with fork; start cutting at narrow end. Hold knife blade at an angle parallel to board.

Cut remaining meat in very thin slices at the same angle. Carving this way cuts with the grain of the flank steak.

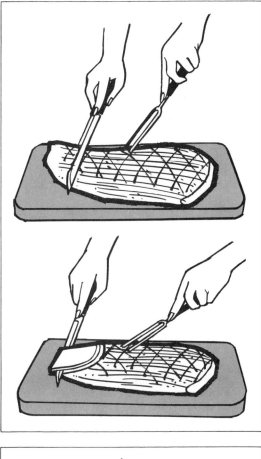

Standing rib roast, *above*, is carved with large end down. Insert fork between ribs. Cut across grain from the fat side to rib bone.

Use tip of knife to cut along rib bones to loosen each slice. Keep as close to bones as possible to make the largest servings.

To lift slice off roast, slide the knife under the slice and steady it with the fork on top. Arrange slices on heated serving platter.

Slice beef brisket, *right*, across grain, 1/8 to 1/4 inch thick. Carve from two sides since grain goes in several directions.

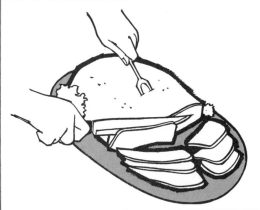

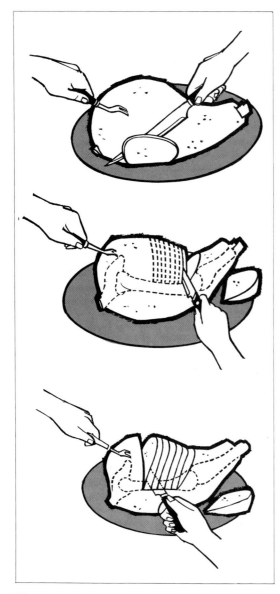

Ham or leg of lamb is carved with shank end on carver's right. Cut a few slices from bottom; wedge slices underneath to steady.

Starting at shank end, cut out and remove small wedge. Slices are then carved perpendicular to the long horizontal leg bone.

Release meat slices by running knife along the leg bone, starting at shank end. Turn the roast on its side and cut additional slices as they are needed.

Remove any stuffing from crown roast. Insert fork between ribs. Carve between ribs beginning where ribs are tied together.

Remove backbone from pork blade loin roast, leaving as much meat on roast as possible. Turn bone side toward carver.

Insert fork in top of the roast. Cut meat servings close along each side of the rib bone. One slice will contain a piece of bone, the next meat slice will be boneless.

Place turkey on board with wing tips folded back. Pull leg out. Cut through meat between thigh and back. Disjoint leg.

For leg, slice meat parallel to bone and under some of the tendons, turning leg. Arrange slices on heated serving platter.

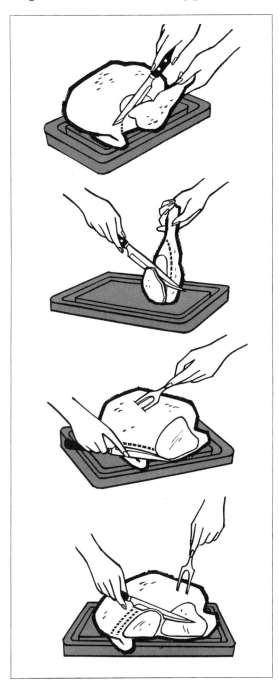

Make a deep horizontal cut into the breast close to wing before carving white meat.

Cut slices from top down to the horizontal cut. Repeat steps with other side of the bird.

CASABA *(kuh sä' buh)*—A winter muskmelon. The mild, sweet casaba is large, globe-shaped, and pointed at the stem end.

Casaba melons are named after the Turkish town of Kassaba which first exported them. The melons in American markets are from California and Arizona.

How to select: Casaba is ripe when the rind is a buttery-yellow color. There should be a softening at the blossom end. The melons are most abundant July to November. Avoid melons with dark, sunken water-soaked spots. They are decaying.

How to store: Leave melons at room temperature if not ripe. Store ripe ones in the refrigerator sealed in a container or in clear plastic wrap. Whole melons keep a week; pieces keep two to four days.

How to prepare: Split casaba open, remove seeds, and slice or cut into pieces of desired size. Chill in the refrigerator.

Casaba melons have soft, creamy-white meat enclosed in a tough, wrinkled, buttery-yellow rind. They have little or no aroma.

How to use: Serve melon as an appetizer, salad, snack, or dessert. Also, use pieces in combination salads. Serve chilled (but not ice cold) with salt, a lemon wedge, or lime wedge. (See also *Melon.*)

Chicken and Ham Salad

- 1⅓ cups uncooked long-grain rice
- ¼ cup French salad dressing
- ¾ cup mayonnaise
- 1 tablespoon finely chopped green onion with tops
- ½ to 1 teaspoon curry powder
- ½ teaspoon dry mustard
- ¾ cup cooked chicken *or* turkey cut in julienne strips
- ¾ cup fully cooked ham cut in julienne strips
- 1 cup sliced raw cauliflower
- ½ 10-ounce package frozen peas, cooked, drained, and chilled
- ½ cup chopped celery
- ½ cup thinly sliced radishes
- 1 casaba melon, well chilled

Cook rice according to package directions; toss with French dressing and chill several hours. Combine mayonnaise, onion, ½ teaspoon salt, dash pepper, curry, and mustard. Add to chilled rice and toss. Add chicken, ham, cauliflower, peas, celery, and radishes; toss.

Using sawtooth cut, halve casaba melon; remove seeds. With grapefruit knife or large sharp-edged spoon, loosen melon meat from rind. Slice meat of each melon half into sections so it can be served with the salad. Fill melon halves with salad. Makes 6 servings.

CASEIN (*kā' sēn*)—A protein found only in milk. Eighty percent of the protein in milk consists of casein. Acid or rennet causes casein to coagulate and form a curd which is the basis for making cheeses.

Casaba doubles as a serving bowl

← Begin mixing Chicken and Ham Salad a day ahead to save last-minute flurry. This main dish is hearty enough to please the men.

CASHEW NUT (*kash' o͞o*)—A small, kidney-shaped nut. Cashew is native to India, Africa, and tropical America. These nuts are the seeds of an applelike fruit which grows on an evergreen tree. Unlike other nuts, they do not have shells.

Today, cashew nuts are imported mainly from India and Brazil. They are sold roasted and salted in cellophane bags, cans, and jars. The nuts can be stored in tightly covered containers in a refrigerator for six months, or in a freezer for one year.

Cashew nuts are ideal for eating out-of-hand as snacks or with drinks. Use as flavor accents or garnishes in salad, casserole, candy, frosting, chicken, and curry. Each nut adds 11 to 14 calories to the daily diet. (See also *Nut.*)

Frosted Cashew Drops

- ½ cup butter or margarine
- 1 cup brown sugar
- 1 egg
- ½ teaspoon vanilla

. . .

- 2 cups sifted all-purpose flour
- ¾ teaspoon baking soda
- ¾ teaspoon baking powder
- ½ teaspoon ground cinnamon
- ¼ teaspoon ground nutmeg
- ⅓ cup dairy sour cream
- 1 cup salted cashew nuts, broken Golden Butter Icing

Cream butter and sugar. Add egg and vanilla; beat well. Sift together flour, soda, baking powder, ¼ teaspoon salt, cinnamon, and nutmeg. Add to creamed mixture alternately with sour cream. Stir in nuts. Drop from teaspoon, 2 inches apart, on greased cookie sheet. Bake at 400° till lightly browned, about 8 to 10 minutes. Remove at once from pan. Cool and frost with Golden Butter Icing. Makes 48 cookies.

Golden Butter Icing: Heat and stir 3 tablespoons butter till browned. Slowly beat in 2 cups sifted confectioners' sugar, 2 tablespoons milk, and 1 teaspoon vanilla.

CASSAVA (*kuh sä' vuh*)—A shrub and the roots of this shrub. Tapioca is made with the starch removed from the root.

CASSEROLE

One-dish combinations for a satisfying main course or hearty meat accompaniment.

Casserole is the name given to both a type of baking dish with a cover and the food that is baked or served in it. In common usage, especially in the United States, any one-dish meal is called a casserole even though it may actually be cooked in a skillet or kettle and transferred to a casserole dish for serving at the table.

The word casserole is derived from *casse*, an early French word for a small pan. It is from this background that foods listed on a menu as being served "en casserole" are single portions in individual dishes such as a ramekin or other small ovenproof container. Larger family-style casseroles contain several servings.

Casserole cooking has been done since man first learned to make earthenware pottery that would withstand the burning coals of an open fire or the heat of a primitive oven. It was natural to prepare satisfying one-dish meals by combining chunks of meat with grasses, herbs, wild fruits, and vegetables. Water was added to prevent the foods from sticking. Man soon discovered that simmering the meat made it tender and juicy. Later, when the earthenware pot had a cover, the liquid did not boil away as quickly and left man with a tasty broth to serve with the meat. This was an early form of stew which today is often served "en casserole." As the years went by, the seasonings in the broth became just as important as the other foods in the stew. As the art of sauce making

developed, the many variations of broth found their place as a necessary ingredient in moistening and seasoning meats, fish, and vegetables in casserole dishes. And, as you know, today many nationalities have special seasoning combinations which have been passed down from mother to daughter for generations.

Choosing the container

Earthenware casseroles of assorted shapes and sizes are still popular for one-dish meals. However, be sure that they are ovenproof. Some types of pottery do not stand up well under sudden contrasts in temperature. Thus, earthenware casseroles are often used as a final serving dish rather than as the actual cooking utensil.

The covered baking dish is the classic casserole in use today. Made of ovenproof glass or ceramic material, it has a close-fitting lid. Some casseroles fit into a frame to hold the dish while serving at the table. Common sizes for this basic glass dish are 10x6x1½ inches (1½ quarts), 12x7½x2 inches (2 quarts), and 13x9x2 inches (3 quarts). Volume and dimensions are usually marked on the bottom of the utensil.

Many skillets are designed for both top-of-the range and oven cooking. If the casserole is to be placed in the oven, the skillet handle should be of heatproof material or be detachable. An electric skillet should not be overlooked as a container. It has one added advantage in that it can be used to prepare food right at the table. Many are colorful and attractive enough for a company buffet meal.

As a rule of thumb, practically any heatproof container makes a satisfactory casserole. If it does not have a lid of its own, you can use aluminum foil. Most recipes

Here's a trio of meaty casseroles

←Burger Skillet Stew features juicy meatballs. Bavarian-Style Stew adds red cabbage. Pioneer Beef Stew wears a pastry top.

Lemon wedges (top) form a golden star atop a seafood casserole. To add more color, dip points in paprika or snipped parsley.

Pinwheel (middle) hot cooked asparagus or overlap slices of green pepper, onion, or tomatoes atop ham or chicken dishes.

Ring top (bottom) with biscuits or dumplings when mixture is bubbly hot. This assures topper will be thoroughly cooked.

specify the size of dish needed. It is a simple matter to measure the volume of a particular pan or dish. Just count the number of cupfuls of water needed to fill it. Or, compare the surface area of two pans, by measuring the length and width from the inside edges. Multiplying width times

length determines surface area in square inches. Remember that the type of baking container will influence the oven temperature or baking time. For example, when switching from a deep container to a shallow one of the same capacity, baking time is shorter for the shallower pan. Recipes generally refer to a baking *pan* when the utensil is metal, and a baking *dish* when it is glass. The reason for the distinction is that the oven temperature is 25° lower when baking in glass utensils.

Casserole combinations

You can prepare casseroles from either cooked or uncooked ingredients, or a combination of both. Generally, start stews with uncooked meat. Ground meats, especially beef, are basic to many types of casserole dishes. Vegetables, which you add later in the cooking time, may be fresh, frozen, or canned. Other recipes taking advantage of canned meats and seafood may rely on canned sauces and vegetables. This way you only need to heat the enticing mixture to blend flavors. Likewise, leftover cooked foods find their way into an assortment of oven-easy meals.

Since most casserole ingredients will be diced or cut up in bite-size pieces, the sauce you use to hold the mixture together is important as a binder. Variations of the classic white sauce are most often used. For convenience sake, you may base the sauce on a canned condensed cream soup such as celery, chicken, or mushroom.

If a white sauce is not compatible with the other foods you're serving, consider making a sauce from a thickened broth or gravy you get from the natural juices of the meat. If the casserole is large in volume, add a bouillon cube or canned broth to augment the sauce.

In a great many tasty casseroles, rice, noodles, macaroni, bread cubes, or potatoes are important ingredients. Their presence gives the dish its one-dish meal status because the starchy complement is included with the meat or cheese. In some cases they can extend the meat ingredient. However, never let the amount of these starch foods outweigh the proportion of the meat and vegetables in the casserole.

Since most casseroles are baked, give some thought to toppings which will brown nicely, yet prevent the surface of the food from drying out. Buttered crumbs, crushed cereal, or potato chips protect the surface and become toasty crisp when the casserole cover is removed during the last few minutes of the baking time.

If you like, add a fancy touch just before the casserole is served. It may be as simple as a few sprigs of parsley or a dash of paprika. Other easy decorating tricks are illustrated on these two pages.

Freezing casseroles

Main-dish casseroles carefully tucked away in the freezer and used within two to four months are work savers on a busy day. Although most meat, vegetable, and sauce combinations freeze well, certain cooking and seasoning tricks will improve the quality of the food.

Generally, it is most satisfactory to freeze the casserole before baking. Otherwise, you are really freezing a leftover which may or may not improve with another heating. In fact, it is wise not to overcook any foods that go into the casserole that require prepreparation. This is especially true of rice, noodles, macaroni, and spaghetti products. They will finish cooking during the time the food is heated before serving. Toppings such as crushed potato chips, crumbs, and cheese should be added near the end of baking time rather than going into the freezer.

It is wise to go easy on the seasonings in a casserole to be frozen. More can always be added later if necessary but some ingredients such as garlic, pepper, and celery intensify during freezing. Experienced cooks will reduce slightly the amounts called for in the recipe.

Use as little fat in the recipe being prepared for the freezer as possible. During reheating it may not blend smoothly.

Remember, a shallow dish will not take as long to thaw and bake as a deep one. If the baking dish is not used, select a freezer container with a wide-top opening so that it's unnecessary to completely thaw the food before removing it from the container for heating. An easy way to remove

Wreathe the casserole (top) in snipped parsley. Place sliced pimiento-stuffed olives in clusters or scatter them over the surface.

Diagonally cut cheese slices (middle) make handy triangles. Point them towards the center or overlap them along the outer edge.

Spread toast with butter (bottom), then sprinkle with garlic salt. Cut toast in small cubes; place on hot casserole before serving.

frozen main dishes from glass canning-freezing jars is to let cool water run on the cap for two or three minutes. This is long enough for the surface of food touching the glass to thaw. Then remove the cap and invert the jar to let the food slide out into the pan to be used for reheating.

Only oven-proof containers can safely be transferred from freezer to hot oven. To save freezer space and free the dish for other use, line the casserole with heavy foil. Allow lengths of foil to extend beyond ends of pan. Fill, then fold the foil over food to seal. Freeze. Remove foil package from dish. Store in freezer. To heat, place in same baking dish, foil and all.

Main-dish meals

Casseroles appear most frequently as the main course of the meal. They may serve as a simple supper for the family or as one of the several entrées on a buffet table.

❖MENU❖

ORIENTAL LUNCHEON
Chopstick Veal Bake
Asparagus Spears   *Spiced Peaches*
Lemon Sherbet   *Ginger Bars*
Hot or *Iced Tea*

Chopstick Veal Bake

    1½ pounds veal steak, cut ½ inch
          thick
      2 tablespoons salad oil
      1 cup chopped onion
    1½ cups sliced celery
      1 cup diced green pepper
      3 tablespoons chopped canned
          pimiento
      ½ cup uncooked long-grain rice
      1 10½-ounce can condensed
          cream of mushroom soup
      1 cup milk
      2 tablespoons soy sauce
      1 3-ounce can chow mein noodles

Cut meat in 2x½-inch strips. Brown in hot oil. Add remaining ingredients *except* noodles. Turn into 2-quart casserole. Cover; bake at 350° for 1¼ to 1½ hours; stir occasionally. Last 5 minutes uncover; top with noodles. Serves 8.

Pioneer Beef Stew

      1 cup large dry lima beans
      1 teaspoon salt
      ¼ cup all-purpose flour
      1 teaspoon salt
      1 teaspoon pepper
      1 pound beef stew meat, cubed
      2 tablespoons shortening
      ½ cup chopped onion
    1½ cups tomato juice
      1 teaspoon salt
      1 small bay leaf
          Dash ground allspice
      1 medium onion, quartered
      3 medium carrots, cut in 1-inch
          slices
      3 stalks celery, cut in 1-inch
          slices
          Pastry Topper

Add beans to 2½ cups water and 1 teaspoon salt and soak overnight. (Or bring mixture to a boil; boil 2 minutes. Remove from heat; let stand covered 1 hour.) Combine flour, 1 teaspoon salt, and pepper in plastic bag; add meat and shake. Brown meat in hot shortening. Add chopped onion, tomato juice, 1 teaspoon salt, bay leaf, and allspice. Cover tightly; simmer 30 minutes. Add beans with liquid, onion, carrots, and celery. Cover, simmer till vegetables are tender, 45 minutes. Remove bay leaf. Thicken stew, if desired. Arrange baked Pastry Topper on hot stew. Serves 6.

Pastry Topper: Prepare 1 stick piecrust mix following package directions. Roll out to 8-inch circle, ¼ inch thick. Cut in 6 wedges. Prick with fork. Bake at 450° 12 to 15 minutes.

Bavarian-Style Stew

Brown 2 pounds beef chuck, cut in 1-inch cubes, in 2 tablespoons hot shortening. Add 3 cups water; 2 medium onions, sliced; 1 tablespoon salt; 1½ teaspoons caraway seed; ¼ teaspoon pepper; and 1 bay leaf. Cover; simmer 1 hour. Add ½ cup vinegar and 2 tablespoons sugar. Cut 1 small head red cabbage in thin wedges; place atop meat.

Cover; simmer till tender, 45 minutes. Remove cabbage to platter. Add ½ cup broken gingersnaps to liquid; bring to boiling, stirring constantly. Makes 6 to 8 servings.

Burger Skillet Stew

1 beaten egg
⅓ cup milk
⅓ cup fine dry bread crumbs
1 envelope spaghetti sauce mix
1 pound ground beef
1 tablespoon shortening
4 medium carrots, peeled and
    cut in 1-inch pieces
½ cup chopped green pepper
1 medium onion, quartered
1 10¾-ounce can beef gravy
¼ cup water

Combine egg, milk, bread crumbs, and *3 table-spoons* of the spaghetti sauce mix. Add ground beef; mix thoroughly. Form mixture into 12 balls; brown in a skillet in hot shortening.

Add carrot pieces, green pepper, and onion to skillet with the meatballs. Blend remaining spaghetti sauce mix with beef gravy and water; pour over meat and vegetables. Simmer, covered, till vegetables are tender, 50 to 60 minutes. Makes 4 to 6 servings.

Family Skillet Supper

¼ cup butter or margarine
3 cups loose-pack frozen
    hash-brown potatoes
¼ cup chopped onion
¼ cup chopped green pepper
¼ teaspoon salt
    Dash pepper
4 slightly beaten eggs
1 12-ounce can luncheon meat
2 ounces sharp process cheese,
    shredded (½ cup)

In 10-inch skillet melt butter. Add hash-brown potatoes, chopped onion, green pepper, salt, and pepper. Stir to combine. Cover; cook over low heat 15 minutes, stirring occasionally. Pour eggs evenly over top of potato mixture.

Cut luncheon meat in 3½x¾-inch sticks; arrange spoke fashion atop eggs. Cover skillet; cook mixture over low heat till eggs are set, about 10 minutes. Sprinkle with shredded cheese; cover till cheese is melted. Cut in wedges. Makes 5 or 6 servings.

Supper ready in 30 minutes? There's no trick to it when frozen hash-brown potatoes, canned luncheon meat, eggs, onion, and sharp cheese team up in a Family Skillet Supper.

Pastry triangles outline a Tuna-Vegetable Pie. Beneath the crust a creamy, herb-seasoned sauce brings together bright carrots and peas, snowy potato cubes, and delicate tuna.

Pork Chops in Spanish Rice

    5 pork chops, ½ inch thick
    2 tablespoons shortening
        • • •
    1 teaspoon salt
    ½ teaspoon chili powder
      Dash pepper
    ¾ cup uncooked long-grain rice
    ½ cup chopped onion
    ¼ cup chopped green pepper
    1 28-ounce can tomatoes
        • • •
    5 green pepper rings
    2 ounces sharp process American
      cheese, shredded (½ cup)

Trim excess fat from chops. In skillet slowly brown pork chops in melted shortening, about 15 to 20 minutes; drain off excess fat.

Combine salt, chili powder, and pepper; sprinkle over meat. Add rice, onion, and chopped green pepper. Pour tomatoes over. Cover and cook over low heat 35 minutes, stirring occasionally. Add green pepper rings and cook till rice and meat are tender, 5 minutes. Sprinkle with cheese. Makes 5 servings.

Tuna-Vegetable Pie

  1½ cups sliced carrots
  1½ cups peeled, cubed potatoes
    ¼ cup butter or margarine
    ¼ cup chopped onion
    2 tablespoons all-purpose flour
    ¼ teaspoon dried rosemary leaves,
      crushed
    1 8-ounce can peas, drained
    2 6½- or 7-ounce cans tuna,
      drained and flaked
    1 stick piecrust mix

Cook carrots and potatoes in small amount of boiling water till tender. Drain, reserving liquid. Add enough milk to make 2 cups.

Melt butter in saucepan. Add onion; cook till tender but not brown. Blend in flour, rosemary, ½ teaspoon salt, and dash pepper. Add milk mixture all at once. Cook, stirring constantly, till mixture is thick and bubbly.

Add vegetables and tuna. Turn into 10x6x 1½-inch dish. Prepare piecrust mix following package directions. Roll out; cut into 6 triangles. Place atop bubbly hot tuna mixture. Bake at 425° 30 to 35 minutes. Serves 6.

Triple Seafood Bake

Stir 1 cup milk, 1 cup light cream, and ⅓ cup dry sherry into one 10½-ounce can condensed cream of mushroom soup.

Add 1⅓ cups uncooked packaged precooked rice; one 4½- or 5-ounce can shrimp, drained and split lengthwise; one 5-ounce can lobster, drained and cut up; one 7½-ounce can minced clams, drained; one 5-ounce can water chestnuts, drained and sliced; one 3-ounce can sliced mushrooms, drained; 1 tablespoon parsley flakes; and ¼ teaspoon instant minced garlic. Turn into 2-quart casserole. Sprinkle with paprika and 2 tablespoons toasted sliced almonds. Dot with 2 tablespoons butter. Bake at 350° for 50 minutes. Makes 6 servings.

Ham Medley

        1 cup chopped celery
        ½ cup chopped green pepper
        ½ cup chopped onion
        ¼ cup butter or margarine, melted
        ¼ cup all-purpose flour
      2½ cups milk
        3 cups cream-style cottage cheese
        4 cups fully cooked ham cut in
            ½-inch cubes
        1 8-ounce package noodles, cooked
            and drained
        2 tablespoons butter or margarine
        ½ cup fine dry bread crumbs

Cook vegetables in butter. Blend in flour, ½ teaspoon salt, and dash pepper. Stir in milk and cheese; cook and stir till boiling. Stir in ham and noodles; turn into 3-quart casserole. Combine remaining ingredients; sprinkle over. Bake at 350° 1 hour. Serves 10 to 12.

Chicken Chow Bake

Combine 2 cups diced cooked chicken; one 10½-ounce can condensed cream of mushroom soup; one 8¾-ounce can pineapple tidbits, drained; 1 cup thinly sliced celery; 2 tablespoons chopped green onion; and 1 teaspoon soy sauce. Add *1 cup* of a 3-ounce can chow mein noodles. Turn mixture into 1½-quart casserole. Top with remaining noodles. Bake at 350° till hot, 45 minutes. Pass soy sauce. Serves 4 to 6.

Macaroni-Cheese Puff

        ½ cup small elbow macaroni
      1½ cups milk
        6 ounces sharp process American
            cheese, shredded
        3 tablespoons butter or margarine
        3 eggs, separated
        1 cup soft bread crumbs
        ¼ cup chopped canned pimiento
        1 tablespoon snipped parsley
        1 tablespoon grated onion
        ¼ teaspoon cream of tartar

Cook macaroni in boiling salted water till tender; drain. Combine milk, cheese, and butter. Cook and stir over low heat till cheese is melted. Beat egg yolks. Stir small amount of hot mixture into beaten yolks. Return to hot mixture; blend thoroughly. Add cooked macaroni, crumbs, pimiento, parsley, and onion.

Beat egg whites with cream of tartar till stiff peaks form. Fold gently into macaroni mixture. Pour into *ungreased* 1½-quart soufflé dish. Bake at 325° till set, about 1 hour. Serves 6.

Side-dish casseroles

Vegetable combinations baked in a casserole bring variety to the menu. Cooked in the oven, they are perfect companions for roasts or braised meats. Butter-baked rice is a pleasing change from baked potatoes to serve with steak or chicken. Experimenting with herbs to season the rice expands the flavor possibilities. Thyme, rosemary, or marjoram head the list, but oregano, curry powder, or saffron can add a foreign influence.

❧MENU❧

SUNDAY CHICKEN DINNER
Perfect Fried Chicken
Baked Rice   Tomato-Zucchini Scallop
Relish Assortment
Chocolate Sundae
Beverage

Baked Rice

        2 teaspoons salt
        1 cup uncooked long-grain rice
        ⅓ cup butter or margarine
            Dash garlic salt
        1 13¾-ounce can chicken
            broth *or* 2 chicken bouillon
            cubes dissolved in 1¾
            cups boiling water
            Finely snipped parsley
        ¼ cup toasted slivered almonds

Combine salt and 2 cups water; bring to boiling and pour over rice. Let stand 30 minutes. Rinse rice with cold water; drain. Melt butter in skillet. Add rice, and cook and stir over medium heat, stirring frequently, till butter is almost absorbed, about 5 minutes. Turn into 1-quart casserole; sprinkle with garlic salt. Pour the broth over the casserole mixture. Bake, covered, at 325° for 45 minutes. Add parsley; fluff with fork. Sprinkle with nuts. Bake, uncovered, 10 minutes. Serves 6 to 8.

Corn and Potato Scallop

        1 17-ounce can whole kernel
            corn, drained
        1 10¼-ounce can frozen cream
            of potato soup, thawed
        ¼ teaspoon salt
            Dash pepper
        2 tablespoons butter or margarine
        ¼ cup shredded Parmesan cheese

Combine corn, soup, salt, and pepper. Turn into greased 1-quart casserole. Dot with butter or margarine; sprinkle Parmesan cheese over top. Bake at 325° until heated through, about 25 minutes. Makes 4 to 6 servings.

Lima-Cheese Bake

Pour boiling water over one 10-ounce package frozen lima beans; break apart. Drain. Blend one 11-ounce can condensed Cheddar cheese soup and ½ cup milk. Add limas, ¾ cup sliced celery, and ¼ cup snipped parsley. Stir in *half* of one 3½-ounce can French-fried onions. Bake at 350° for 35 minutes. Trim with remaining onions; bake 10 minutes. Makes 6 servings.

Tomato-Zucchini Scallop

        2 small zucchini squash, sliced
        1 medium onion, thinly sliced
        2 small tomatoes, peeled and
            sliced
        1 cup plain croutons
        1 teaspoon salt
            Pepper
                •   •   •
        1 tomato, cut in wedges
        4 ounces sharp natural Cheddar
            cheese, shredded (1 cup)

In a 1½-quart casserole, layer *half* of the zucchini, onion, sliced tomatoes, and croutons. Season with ½ *teaspoon* of the salt and dash pepper. Repeat layers. Top with tomato wedges. Cover and bake at 350° for 1 hour. Uncover and sprinkle with cheese. Return to oven till cheese melts. Serve in sauce dishes. Makes 6 servings.

Festive Celery Casserole

        4 cups celery cut in ¼-inch slices
        2 tablespoons butter or margarine
        1 10½-ounce can condensed cream
            of celery soup
        2 tablespoons milk
        2 tablespoons chopped canned
            pimiento
                •   •   •
        ½ cup finely crushed round cheese
            crackers (12 crackers)
        1 tablespoon butter or margarine,
            melted

In a saucepan cook celery, covered, in the 2 tablespoons butter till tender, 15 to 20 minutes. Stir in soup, milk, and chopped pimiento. Pour into a 1-quart casserole.

Combine cracker crumbs and melted butter or margarine. Sprinkle crumb mixture over casserole. Bake at 350° for 30 minutes or till heated through. Makes 4 to 6 servings.

Oven-easy vegetables

Look to the oven for tempting vegetables → such as Tomato-Zucchini Scallop and Stuffed Acorn Squash. (See *Acorn Squash* for recipe.)

CASSIA (*kash′ uh, kas′ ē-*)—A name used in the spice trade for several varieties of cinnamon bark native to China, Indo-China, and Indonesia. The buds and flowers are sometimes used in pickling.

Cassia is also a generic term for certain leguminous plants possessing medicinal properties. (See also *Cinnamon*.)

CASSOULET (*ka suh lā′*)—A casserole specialty of the Toulouse region of France. The basic ingredient is stewed white beans to which pork, lamb, duck, and special sausages are added. Except for the white beans, the other ingredients differ in kind and amount in various towns.

CASTOR SUGAR—The British name to designate finely granulated sugar.

CATFISH—A freshwater fish native to the lakes and streams of the Great Lakes region and the Mississippi river with its many tributaries. The whiskerlike sensory barbels on the jaws lend the name catfish. Though the fish may weigh more than 100 pounds, average market size is from one to 20 pounds, dressed, ready-to-cook.

Catfish meat is firm and flaky with a delicate flavor. The small-sized panfish are favorites of anglers, but catfish are important commercially, too. Bullhead, channel, blue, or yellow catfish are names by which the fish is known. (See also *Fish*.)

CATSUP, CATCHUP, KETCHUP—A spicy, thick, slightly-sweet sauce served with meat and fish or used an an ingredient in main dishes. The most familiar is tomato. It may have a smoke or other flavoring.

Best Tomato Catsup

    1½ teaspoon whole cloves
    1½ inches broken stick cinnamon
      1 teaspoon celery seed
      1 cup white vinegar
          • • •
      8 pounds tomatoes, cored and
           quartered (about 25 medium)
      1 medium onion, chopped
     ¼ teaspoon cayenne pepper
      1 cup sugar

In small saucepan combine cloves, stick cinnamon, celery seed, and white vinegar. Cover; bring to a boil. Remove from heat; let stand. In a large kettle combine tomatoes, onion, and cayenne. Bring to boil; cook 15 minutes, stirring occasionally. Sieve mixture.

Add sugar to tomato juice. Bring to boil; *simmer* briskly till mixture is reduced by half (measure depth with ruler at start and end) about 1½ to 2 hours. Strain spice-vinegar mixture into tomato mixture; discard spices. Add 4 teaspoons salt. Simmer till of desired consistency, about 30 minutes. Stir often.

Fill hot pint jars to within ½ inch of top; adjust lids. Process in boiling water bath 5 minutes (count time after water returns to the boiling point). Makes 2 pints.

Sweet-Sour Stew

      2 pounds beef stew meat, cubed
     ¼ cup all-purpose flour
     ¼ cup shortening
     ½ cup catsup
     ¼ cup brown sugar
     ¼ cup vinegar
      1 tablespoon Worcestershire sauce
      1 teaspoon salt
      1 cup chopped onion
      6 large carrots, cut in
           ¾-inch pieces

Coat meat with mixture of flour, 1 teaspoon salt, and dash pepper. In large skillet brown meat well in hot shortening. Combine 1 cup water, catsup, brown sugar, vinegar, Worcestershire, and salt. Stir into browned meat; add onion. Cover; cook over low heat for 45 minutes, stirring occasionally. Add carrots. Cook till meat and carrots are tender, about 45 minutes. Makes 6 to 8 servings.

CAUDLE—A hot spiced drink given in past years to invalids. The recipe is English in origin and has numerous variations. One such variation consists of strong tea diluted with wine, to which spices are added. The concoction is further enriched with beaten egg yolk. Another variation with a base of cereal gruel makes use of beer or wine, sugar, and spices and is made either with or without egg.